PRAISE FOR
WELCOME TO THEOLOGICAL FIELD EDUCATION!

An indispensable read for students, field educators, faculty, CPE Supervisors, mentors/supervisors and congregations involved in contextual education and the pastoral formation process. Eleven nationally known, seasoned scholars and educators present rich and sobering elements, detailed examples based on theory, scripture, and research for students and educators. This book gets you in the proper frame for understanding the how and why of theological field education, and introduces you to the finer points of equipping one as a reflective pastoral practitioner.
—*Richard [Dick] Cunningham, Assistant Professor, Director Contextual Education, School of Theology and Ministry, Seattle University*

Welcome to Theological Field Education provides a solid introduction to the multifaceted discipline of training seminarians to become skilled pastors. Written by experienced FE professionals, it is an insightful, systematic, and theologically sound manual that I believe is a must-read for those beginning the challenging enterprise of theological field education.
—*The Rev. Deborah K. Davis, Director of Field Education, Princeton Theological Seminary*

The distinction between field work (learning how to perform tasks) and field education (growing as people and professionals) is at the heart of this insightful collection of essays. Personal experiences, case studies, and practical exercises combine with theoretical expertise to illustrate the importance of placing the functions and practices of ministry within the larger framework of the formation of the whole person for effective preparation of candidates for ministry.

—Randy A. Nelson, Professor Emeritus of Contextual Education, Luther Seminary

Seminary students and supervisor-mentors preparing to embark on the journey of service-learning will find in these chapters a wealth of knowledge that will prepare them for the experience. The authors of each chapter speak directly to Field Education participants out of their area of expertise, so that by the end of the volume, a reader will have had the opportunity to learn from some of the finest Field Educators across North America.

—P. Alice Rogers, Assistant Professor in the Practice of Congregational Leadership, Candler School of Theology

WELCOME TO
THEOLOGICAL FIELD EDUCATION!

WELCOME TO THEOLOGICAL FIELD EDUCATION!

Matthew Floding, General Editor

Herndon, Virginia
www.alban.org

Copyright © 2011 by The Alban Institute. All rights reserved. This material may not be photocopied or reproduced in any way without written permission. Go to www.alban.org/permissions.asp or write to the address below.

The Alban Institute
2121 Cooperative Way, Suite 100
Herndon, VA 20171

Unless otherwise noted, all Scripture quotations are from the New Revised Standard Version of the Bible, © 1989, Division of Christian Education of the National Council of Churches of Christ in the United States of America, and are used by permission.

Cover design by Tobias Becker, Bird Box Design.

Library of Congress Cataloging-in-Publication Data

Welcome to theological field education! / Matthew Floding, general editor.
    p. cm.
 Includes bibliographical references.
 ISBN 978-1-56699-407-1
 1. Pastoral theology--Fieldwork. I. Floding, Matthew, 1955-
 BV4164.5.W94 2010
 253.071'55--dc22
                        2010044050

Contents

Foreword		ix
Preface		xiii
CHAPTER 1	What Is Theological Field Education? *Matthew Floding*	1
CHAPTER 2	The Art of Supervision and Formation *Charlene Jin Lee*	17
CHAPTER 3	Ministerial Reflection *Emily Click*	31
CHAPTER 4	The Use of Case Studies in Field Education *Tim Sensing*	45
CHAPTER 5	The Power of Reflecting with Peers *Donna R. Duensing*	65
CHAPTER 6	The Forming Work of Congregations *Lee Carroll*	75
CHAPTER 7	Self-Care and Community *Jaco Hamman*	101
CHAPTER 8	Ministerial Ethics *Barbara Blodgett*	115

CHAPTER 9 Language and Leadership 133
Lorraine Ste-Marie

CHAPTER 10 Considerations for Cross-Cultural Placement 155
Joanne Lindstrom

CHAPTER 11 Assessment and Theological Field Education 169
Sarah B. Drummond

Notes 191

Bibliography 201

Contributors 205

Foreword

Not so long ago only a few individuals found careers in theological field education. Those who did most often did it accidentally, for there was no established vocation to enter and certainly none to prepare for. Occasioned by students working in part-time ministry jobs to pay the bills while attending seminary or theological school, theological field education was born in the middle of the last century, when neither students nor faculty thought of the "field work" jobs as part of the educational process.

Eventually the Association of Theological Schools (ATS) included field education in its standards for accreditation, but even so, as late as a generation ago, most field educators came into their positions somewhat serendipitously, and for most of them field education was a way station. There were always a few who didn't—George Hunter, Don Beisswenger, Tjaard Hommes, Doran McCarty, Shelley Finson, and Lynn Rhodes, to name a few—and they were pioneers in theological field education, both its practice and its research. But I still have somewhere stacks of file folders containing the yellowing, typewritten articles and handouts that many of us cobbled together back then to teach students and supervisors the art and rubrics.

How things have changed! Many more theological field educators now come to the work as an intentional vocation and one in which they intend to stay. Readers of this book are fortunate beneficiaries of this new era. Leading theological field educators, scholar/practitioners I would call them, throughout North America have brought their insights, scholarship, and experience to bear on the making of this volume. The authors have written significant essays on a coherent set of topics, and the result is a cogent guide for field educators, students, and supervisors.

More about the chapters shortly. But before leaving field education's history, I want to revisit a discussion that arose during theological field education's maturation that has implications for this volume. Once field education was firmly established as an educational requirement and had also become a clear vocational destination, the question sometimes arose, is field education a discipline or a methodology? Another way of asking the question, is to ask: how is field education a discipline unto itself? That is, is it a field of study with its own knowledge base to be taught and studied? Or is field education a way of educating theological students that relies on and integrates various fields? If it is a discipline, then theological field education would reach its full maturity only when it became a field of study in which aspiring field educators would earn an advanced degree as preparation for teaching in the discipline. If it is not its own discipline, then field educators might be educated in a variety of relevant disciplines. Some saw the idea of a recognized discipline and the concomitant establishment of degree programs in field education to be the final frontier in credibility. Others, however, worried about further fracturing theological education with yet another discipline at a time when interdisciplinarity was gaining a foothold in North American education generally, and especially because ministry is an interdisciplinary vocation to its bones. Currently the question is settled, if not philosophically then at least de facto, in that most field educators, and the contributors to this volume are examples, are educated in fields such as religious education, pedagogy, pastoral care and counseling, psychology, practical theology, ethics, narrative theory, and homiletics. The result is a set of chapters marked by both coherence and rich variety as each author contributes his or her strengths and particular perspectives to service in their common vocation of theological field education.

Welcome to Theological Field Education will be a welcome text in courses for field education students and courses for field education supervisors. A scan of the table of contents reveals a relatively complete set of topics ranging from just what field education is; to the nuts and bolts of reflection, planning and assessment, and using case studies; to the considerations of ethics, language, and self-care; to the roles of cross cultural placements, congregations, and peers. Long gone are the stacks of file folders with their yellowed and typed pages.

The best part, though, is found in the reading of the chapters. Each sparkles with depth, nuance, and perspective and showcases the special qualifications and passions of its author. The winsome chapter about supervision and formation by Charlene Jin Lee captures something of what the whole book itself pulls off. She says,

> Many years later I realized that the formation of a piano virtuoso was about far more than training. One teacher, instead of simply watching me practice, allowed me to watch her practice. Before I learned a new piece, she would bring her own copy of the music, which was full of penciled notations, the edges of the sheets rolled and frayed. She would sit at the center of the piano bench and begin to play the piece. Sometimes her eyes were closed as if she were in a dream, sometimes her eyes focused intensely at the measures of the printed music. Her body would sway as if to dance, and her face expressed something inward she could not hide. I watched my teacher interact with the text of the music; she would then watch as I tried out my own interactions with the text. I discovered and rediscovered that the activity of pressing wooden keys with my fingers was more than merely this. It was remembering the composition, creating sound, and evoking interpretation. (22)

What we are treated to is nothing less than each author's copy of the music with its "penciled annotations, the edges of the sheets rolled and frayed." The reader gets to watch each of the authors play the piece. In field education, whichever of the roles—teacher, student, supervisor—they inhabit, they will try out their own interaction with its text. With these authors at their side they will discover and rediscover the great joy of "pressing the keys" and "remembering the composition, creating sound, and evoking interpretation," that is, they will discover and rediscover the great joy at the heart of their work.

Dudley C. Rose
Associate Dean, Ministry Studies
Harvard Divinity School

Preface

Now there are varieties of gfts, but the same Spirit . . .
—1 CORINTHIANS 12:4

Theological field education is informed by many theoretical fields, and its practitioners come to practice their art richly informed not only by these but also by their service in the church and other forms of ministry. This rich matrix of educational backgrounds and deep ministry commitments engenders among field educators an intense curiosity about how adults learn and are formed for ministry. Prior engagements in ministry have also formed field educators to be inclined toward collaboration, since experientially we know the truth of the apostle Paul's words, "To each is given the manifestation of the Spirit for the common good" (1 Cor. 12:7).

This, in fact, has been my experience in twelve years as a field educator and being privileged to partner with others through the professional organization, the Association for Theological Field Education (ATFE). I marvel at the giftedness and passion of its members and have benefited profoundly from their generosity.

The genesis of this book is grounded in this experience. I reasoned, Why not introduce theological field education to students, supervisor-mentors, and other participants by asking leaders in the field to speak from an area of their research interest and passion? It was my delightful experience then to invite talented colleagues, from whom I was eager to learn, to contribute to this book. This means that readers will encounter authors from a variety of educational backgrounds and Christian traditions, each expert in his or her topic. I also wish to thank the research and publications committee of ATFE for a grant to launch the project.

The Alban Institute's mission to build up congregations and their leaders to be agents of grace and transformation made them a superb partner in this project. When better to build up leaders than when they begin their formal ministerial education?

    Matthew Floding
    Chair, Steering Committee of the Association for Theological
        Field Education
    Western Theological Seminary

1
What Is Theological Field Education?

MATTHEW FLODING

Welcome to theological field education! Field education is an opportunity for you to develop ministry skills, practice ministerial reflection, discern your call, experience professional collegiality, and undergo personal transformation. This is what field education is about—and more. Seminaries and divinity schools value students actually doing ministry so that they can integrate ministry theory and practice. For many students, the ministry setting will be a congregation and for others a hospital, campus ministry, or faith-based agency. No matter what ministry God is calling you to, field education will be a significant part of your preparation. Field education offers you a place to practice ministry and spaces to reflect on it so that you can grow toward competency in ministry.

Not Always So

While today every theological seminary or divinity school in the United States and Canada accredited by the Association of Theological Schools must provide for field education, this has not always been the case. I recently spoke with Pastor John Smith, who graduated from seminary in 1952, about his ministry experiences during seminary.[1] Back then, students initiated their own experience by volunteering at a local congregation to teach, preach, and assist the pastor during the school year. In the summer, students sought paying summer assignments to broaden their experience. One summer the soon-to-be-pastor ministered in rural South Dakota. Since he didn't have a car, he hitchhiked to each of his pastoral call destinations. He was paid fifteen dollars per week. It was an amazing experience, even call-defining for him, as he went on to a forty-plus year ministry in rural churches. But students received no academic credit for their labor, just experience and a modest paycheck. Such labors were often referred to as "field work."

Seminary faculty, in the late 1950s and early '60s, took note that students like John Smith entered the classroom energized by their experience and they asked good questions—lots of them. Naturally, faculty seized upon the opportunity to weave these experiences into the classroom and later into the curriculum as "field education." This move formally acknowledged that growth through practicing ministry was not simply work but educational. Impetus for further integrating field education into seminary curriculums throughout North America came in 1966 as a result of a study, "Education for Ministry," sponsored by the Association of Theological Schools and conducted by Charles Feilding, a professor of pastoral theology at Trinity College, Toronto.[2] Feilding, critical of his own field, noted, "The trouble in the practical departments is the widespread tendency to replace practice with lectures about practice."[3] He went on to argue in the study that an organized field education program was essential for theological education, for "nothing short of this can be taken seriously as professional education."[4] Since the publication of "Education for Ministry," seminaries and divinity schools began to require students to engage in well-coordinated field education that includes theological reflection on the practice of ministry with supervisor-mentors and peers. In this book, this student-centered process is referred to as *ministerial reflection*.

Student Growth and Transformation

In fact, let's start with you. You will be investing many personal resources and three or more years of time preparing for your calling. What are some factors you might consider as you enter this transforming educational process? You come from a rich and interesting matrix of family, educational, personal growth, and ministry experiences with a good deal of formation having already taken place. God has already invested a great deal in your life. In the midst of all of this, God spoke to you in a way that led you to seminary. As you listen to your fellow students, you will learn that each has a unique story to tell related to this matter of call. Don't feel overly anxious if you aren't certain at the beginning of your seminary experience about what God has in mind for you. Here is one thing you can count on: God seems pleased to use the process of seminary, and field education in particular, to clarify students' sense of call. This is what students report in self-evaluations as they reflect on their field education experience. For example, here Stephen reflects on an experience in his self-evaluation after his first semester of field education.

> One moment this semester that I felt particularly accompanied by God's presence occurred while teaching an adult education class. Following a showing of an International Justice Mission film on modern-day slavery, I explored their questions. After researching and preparing, I responded to one question with an explanation that our calling is to witness to the kingdom of God. Though we cannot make God's kingdom come, we do pray for it and act in ways that affirm how it will someday be. While "proclaiming" this good news, I felt a sense of energy and peace. While I judge myself to be a better writer than speaker, I believe the Spirit is building confidence in my speaking abilities.

For most students, entering seminary is a new beginning, and many feel a bit displaced. You may have moved across country to attend a denominational seminary or a divinity school whose ethos was attractive to you. Perhaps you have left a career and you and your family feel a bit like Abraham and Sarah going to a place that you have never been before. Nevertheless, your confidence can be that God the caller, as with Sarah and Abraham, will lead to the place "I will show you" (Gen. 12:1).

Perhaps an insight from the work of Erik Erikson can also encourage you. Recall Erikson's psychosocial theory from your general psychology class. In his schema, we negotiate different challenges at each of the stages of development, paying special attention to social cues as we grow. When we enter a new experience, especially a new community, we renegotiate, in a sense, the earlier stages. For example, when you first entered the seminary environment and met your seminary colleagues, perhaps at an orientation experience, you first needed to establish whether you could trust (versus mistrust) this environment. If you determined you could, you ventured further, disclosing more of your ideas and feelings and gauging your peers' and professors' responses (initiative versus guilt). According to Erikson, we then move on to the adolescent stage when we must negotiate "identity versus role confusion."[5] Finding your place by moving through these stages will hopefully take you from feeling displaced to thinking, "I love my seminary community!"

Erikson's insights also inform how field education might help you understand the contours of your call. Social feedback is an important facet of field education. Field education provides hospitable ministry environments where you will be encouraged to try on various ministry roles so that you can practice ministry, receive helpful feedback, and enjoy space to reflect on your experience. You will discover your ministry identity by doing ministry. Remember, it is you, all that you are by nature and by grace, whom God is calling to ministry. No other. This is illustrated well in a Hasidic tale. Rabbi Zusya, when he was an old man, said, "In the coming world, they will not ask me, 'Why were you not Moses?' They will ask me, 'Why were you not Zusya?'"[6]

Field education also allows you to make adjustments to your mental map of the world. Your family of origin, education, and religious and other life experiences, as well as regional and larger cultural forces, have shaped your way of looking at the world. From all of these experiences you have formed an internal map of how the world works and how best to navigate it.[7] It allows you to make sense of things and at times cope with extra challenging experiences. Everyone else has formed a map too, and in seminary you will learn that each of our maps is a bit different, and that given our cognitive limits no one of us has the perfect map. Some differences will appear in the classroom, some in your ministry settings, others elsewhere. Often, you will feel uncomfortable, perhaps even disturbed, about these differences. You might feel your dis-ease with a situation even before you can name it. It is a ministerial skill to understand, even appreciate another's way of framing the world in which he or she participates. Can you be flexible and patient enough to discern another's perspective? One illustration for learning to adjust my map comes from my first weeks of being married. I soon discovered that Marcia, my wife, and my mother did things differently. One example: My mother grew up in a Great Depression farm family that was very careful with budget and meal planning. Leftovers were built into the week's menu. This carried over into my childhood home. Marcia grew up in a solid middle-class engineer and teacher's home that had a bit more freedom financially. When it came to groceries there was greater flexibility. That was her experience and she brought it into our marriage. I stressed over whether our budget could handle it. In the end—and for the good of the marriage—I had to acknowledge that both Marcia and my mom lived within their means and fed their families, and they both did it well. I needed to adjust my map. The point is that if you enter your seminary experience and your field education placement with a spirit of generosity and as a learner, it will be a rich experience indeed, and you will learn to appreciate the diversity of perspectives around you.

One more thing about you. Field education empowers you as a learner. This is one of those instances in your life when it is about you. As an adult learner you have gained from both formal education and the lessons that life teaches. You may also know what you want to learn. Don't be afraid to speak candidly with your field educator and your ministry supervisor about your learning goals. Here is an acronym to help you identify them: NICE.

- N is for *needs*. Do not be afraid to spell out what it is you need in order to achieve your learning goals and objectives. It will be an encouragement to your ministry supervisor and your field educator to know how they can tailor the learning opportunity to address the needs you have identified.
- I is for *interests*. Let your ministry supervisor and field educator know what you are interested in, the more specific the better. Each is committed to providing space for you to explore your ministry interests.
- C is for *concerns*. You may at times have concerns about your field placement. Your supervisor-mentor is the first person to speak with since he or she wants the field education experience to go well. However, if you need help thinking through how you might speak to the concern, meet with your field educator, who is an expert at this kind of thing.
- E is for *expectations*. Make sure that you and your supervisor-mentor are operating with the same expectations. Your learning covenant or learning and serving contract, a written document in which you and your ministry supervisor spell out learning goals and objectives for a unit of field education, provides one opportunity to discuss and define these.

Even though you are an adult learner, let's admit that training to become a professional in a new arena means that there are things you do not know. Let's add H for *humility* to the acronym. Invite your ministry supervisor to lead you into experiences that you might never think of. Much of ministry during the week is never seen by the congregation and requires a wide range of skills: time management, crisis intervention, counseling, scholarship, administration, mediation, and so forth. For example, how does a pastor conduct a staff meeting at church with the part-time youth minister, the custodian, the administrative assistant, and the volunteer music minister? That requires skill. Your mentor possesses a wealth of knowledge on these and many other subjects because she or he lives with these challenges week in and week out. In fact, as Craig Dykstra writes in *For Life Abundant*, "To be a good pastor, you have to be very smart in lots of really interesting ways."[8] This wisdom is yours for the asking.

Place and Space

The field education director at your theological school has cultivated a network of congregations to serve as internship sites. You may enter a congregation that has recently adopted this role or a congregation whose identity has been connected to the seminary since the seminary's founding. Be assured, congregations in each of these settings take their role with utmost seriousness and work to be the best teaching congregation they can be. Clergy, staff, and members of each congregation understand that the leader they are training might someday be their own minister.

Field education is not a one-size-fits-all proposition, however. Your sense of call may be directing you toward a noncongregational setting. Your field educator has also developed a number of internship sites that allow students to explore call outside the walls of the congregation. Hospitals, prisons, campus ministries, nursing homes, restorative justice programs, and myriads of other faith-based agencies may be options for you—depending on your seminary's context. You may wish to spend time in an alternative context just to stretch your vision of ministry.

Supervisor-mentors have been oriented to the field education program and receive in-service training to help them grow in their supervision skills. You soon will enter a hospitable place to practice ministry, you will serve under a skilled supervisor-mentor, and you will take on the role of a ministerial leader and be doing the work of ministry. This place to practice ministry and space to reflect on it is where the experiential component of formation for ministry can flower. In the early part of the twentieth century, one of the parents of adult education theory, Eduard Lindeman at Columbia University, wrote, "The resource of highest value in adult education is the learner's experience."[9] Raw experience doesn't guarantee that you or I will learn, however. Field education will leverage your experience for transformational learning. Experiential learning can involve both successes and mistakes. In a delightful essay, Joseph Levine, an education professor at Michigan State University, observes, "Recently someone suggested to me that we learn more from our mistakes than our successes. How does that person know? I can think of lots of times when I haven't learned from either! . . . The key is that we have the power to learn from our mistakes. And the way we exercise this power is by taking time to reflect."[10]

Lindeman and Levine underscore the two most important components of learning in your internship setting: experience in the practice of ministry and reflection on that practice. Sometimes this is referred to as the action-reflection model of learning.[11] Your active participation in ministry will provide plenty of data for reflection, hopefully, with many stories of effectiveness. But when mistakes happen—they surely will—and you have time to reflect on what took place and what happened within you, you can follow Levine's sage advice: "Reflection takes on its most powerful form when we're able to 'return to the scene of the crime' and act again. This suggests that to really learn from a mistake takes not only time to reflect but also the opportunity to try out the results of our reflection."[12]

Through ministerial reflection in regular meetings with your supervisor-mentor you will be able to reflect on your experiences—successes and not so successful experiences—and turn these into powerful growth opportunities. You may also have a lay support team that is praying for you and will meet regularly with you to reflect on these experiences. Your supervisor-mentor has been trained in methods of ministerial reflection, and you will also receive training in ministerial reflection in your field education companion courses. Many field education programs also provide peer reflection groups in which to process your ministry experiences using a variety of tools. Rich insight into self and ministry can be gleaned from any number of sources. In fact, it may be best to think of your field education program as a *mentoring environment*.[13] Be alert to all of the wonderful resource people God may use in your formation for ministry.

God has staked a claim in our formation experience. Paul writes to promote confidence in God's commitment to our formation in Christ: "The one who began a good work among you will bring it to completion" (Phil. 1:6). The psalmist too confesses, "For it was you who formed my inward parts; you knit me together in my mother's womb. I praise you, for I am fearfully and wonderfully made" (Ps. 139:13–14a). The psalmist speaks of "being made in secret" (v. 15). Our formation from creation to our life's end is a work of grace that God has initiated by the Spirit and in which we are called to participate. Something deep and even mysterious is going on in formation for ministry. Field education can empower us to discover who we are and give us and others glimpses of who we may become. Can you be open to God's surprises through your field education experience?

Perhaps this prayer offered in worship by a seminarian in his field education placement might become your own as you embark on your seminary journey.

> O Lord God, Creator above us, Spirit within us, Lord ahead of us, open us to yourself, that we may become transparent to ourselves. Make us masters of ourselves, that we may be the eager servants of others.
> In the name of Jesus Christ, we bless you for the gift of our lives.[14]

A Word to Supervisor-Mentors

You and the people you serve in your ministry context have been granted a sacred trust: the formation of a soon-to-be-minister. In partnership with the seminary or divinity school, you function as a kind of off-campus faculty member in a laboratory setting with a class size of one or two. Thank you for taking on this holy responsibility.

Seminary and divinity school students in North America have long benefited from the wisdom of experienced ministers. In the North American context, before the first stand-alone seminary came into being (New Brunswick Theological Seminary was established in 1794) and for some generations after in various traditions, pastors mentored young apprentices.

In a small-town New England parish dating back to those days, two pastors whose tenures spanned one hundred years in that one parish continually had students living with them, studying Greek and Hebrew, and catching a sense of what ministry was all about before going on to their more formal studies at Harvard. The stipends of these colonial pastor-supervisors were apportioned by the General Court of Massachusetts and included twelve pounds sterling, two barrels of cider, a keg of rum, and ten cords of wood. Life was considerably more primitive then. Now one cannot help but marvel over the commitment of those clergy to serving as teachers, mentors, and tutors in the theological education of those days.[15] (A disclaimer: you may or may not receive such a generous stipend for your service today!)

There is something romantic about the picture of students living in the home of their mentor. On further reflection, you and I could probably imagine a number of challenges that this living and learning arrangement might bring. It does serve to remind us of the extraordinary hospitality required of supervisor-mentor and the congregation. In an in-service training for supervisor-mentors, Charlene Jin Lee, professor of Christian education at San Francisco Seminary, underscored this notion. "We form people whom we supervise/mentor as students experience us. They learn who we are . . . so we must be authentically present for formation to take place. As we assume the posture of one who is learning and relearning, we provide space where struggles and questions can be voiced."[16] Hospitality is important, but not the only requisite for a positive learning experience. Lee connects hospitality and authenticity in the learning context and relationship. Supervision and mentoring will require of you a good deal of intellectual, emotional, and spiritual energy. You may even do a bit of coaching.

The following insights could come from any sport or from anyone coaching musicians or actors. The traits described in a *USA Hockey* magazine article addressing coaches at the youth level speak directly to the character of supervision and mentoring.[17] Let's consider how these apply to a new relationship with a student intern.

- *Humility*: "Every coach wants to win but not at the expense of skill development." In other words, a great supervisor-mentor does an ego check and focuses on the joys and satisfactions of seeing growth and development in another.
- *Compassion*: "Great coaches take time to know their players on and off the ice." Supervisor-mentors can recall their own preparation for ministry and so invest a great deal of energy listening to their intern, showing respect and empathy for them and their life situation.
- *Communication*: "Great coaches are able to deliver criticism and praise in a way that players will take to heart." This kind of helpful communication is grounded in an understanding of how this particular intern hears and receives feedback in order to grow.
- *Passion*: "When a coach has a passion for the game and the team, it makes the experience positive for everyone involved." Your love for ministry can be contagious. Share it!
- *Leadership*: "Great coaches give their teams direction and motivation to help them to reach their goals." As a professional, you possess an enormous amount of training, experience, and tacit knowledge of what ministry is about. As the leader in the relationship, you can guide and direct your intern into important experiences as well as negotiate around his or her personal interests to ensure the student experiences a breadth of leadership practice upon which to reflect.

Clearly your disposition as supervisor-mentor is extremely significant to the effectiveness of this formational experience. This is not to diminish the importance of the student's disposition entering the field education placement or the church's or ministry's disposition receiving and hosting the intern. Making this level of commitment to a student's professional development, however, is not easy for a number of reasons. First, you may already feel overcommitted. If so, the temptation may be to view this supervision-mentoring commitment as "one more thing" on your planner. This will likely keep you from giving your student the attention you would wish you could to support their learning needs. Second, it's easy to succumb to the temptation to view an intern as free or low-cost labor. It works something like this: "Our ministry has needs and the student needs experience—a match made in heaven! Plug them in." Field education is primarily about the student's formation for ministry and only secondarily about the needs of the placement. Third, doing ministry as a team sport is challenging. The skill of team leadership is something that each of us pastors has had to learn, or is still learning, often the hard way, once we acknowledged that we are not uber-ministers. We learned to trust others and to delegate. We also learned that the body of Christ is an empowering metaphor for ministry, that each part has value and needs to be called into service, affirmed, and celebrated. In this regard, we may have even claimed Max De Pree's metaphor, leadership jazz, recognizing that we as leaders have a responsibility to empower young "musicians" not only to play according to the requirements of the band and the music but also to trust them enough to call them out for exhilarating moments of improvisation in the spotlight.[18] Your intern's admiration and appreciation for your efforts will only grow over time as he or she learns how challenging the work of supervision and mentoring are.

Over several years the field education team at Western Theological Seminary asked our students the same question: "What does your mentor *do* that is helpful in your formation?"[19] The research we have conducted among our students suggests the following are marks of a good mentor:

- He listens and affirms well.
- She is available and consistent.
- She lets me bring questions that concern me.
- He lets me try new things, even experiment.
- They [pastoral staff] genuinely care about me.
- He wants me to experience all aspects of ministry.
- I was asked what I wanted to learn and was taken seriously.
- He pays attention to both the professional and the personal identity stuff.
- She pushes me to be self-reflective.
- She offers encouraging and specific feedback.
- He took me along and introduced me to everyone; I felt welcomed.
- He challenges me to see alternative approaches to ministry.
- He advocates for my well-being in the system.

Most of what appears on this list is second nature to you, because it is at the core of your pastoral identity. Other items will require effort on your part. You can perhaps recall how you were both anxious and eager as you entered your field education experience. All of us wanted a supervisor-mentor to make us feel welcome and to convey that our internship really mattered to her or him. As I recall my own field education experience, I think I was a bit like my cocker spaniel, Cynder: I was eager to please, and a little affirmation went a long way. Perhaps one helpful way to frame the work of supervision and mentoring is to remember that you are participating in God's shaping of this person's call, a minister who will be your colleague for life.

Earlier in this chapter, I asked students to recall Erik Erikson's developmental theory related to identity resolution. Interestingly, professionals in student development have long wrestled with the identity resolution component of Erikson's theory in order to shape cocurricular programming such as various clubs, volunteer opportunities, and competitive athletics. Research findings indicate that identity resolution is affected positively by a learning environment characterized by

- experiences that help the individual clarify her or his interests, skills, and attitudes;
- experiences that aid the individual in making commitments;
- experimenting with varied roles;
- making choices;
- enjoying meaningful achievement;
- freedom from excessive anxiety in the performance environment;
- taking time for reflection and introspection.[20]

Neither you nor your congregation can control the learning outcomes in your student's internship. One student may become a better preacher when given the opportunity to practice and reflect with a mentor; another, a better caregiver; another, a better team builder; and so on. What you as supervisor-mentor can do is create a hospitable learning environment and give permission to a student to practice ministry. To paraphrase MIT educator Donald Schön, he or she must begin pastoring in order to learn to pastor.[21] In practice, this means that you step back so that your student can step up. This learning-rich environment fosters formation for ministry and vocational clarity.

Formation for ministry is especially challenging at this time in the church's life. An Alban Institute special report on the impact of the Lilly Foundation's Transition into Ministry initiative, *Becoming a Pastor: Reflections on the Transition into Ministry,* underscores the challenge: "While the Corinth of Paul's time or the London of Wesley's era experienced their own forms of cosmopolitanism and change, the environments of the early 21st century make the forming of ministers an especially daunting task."[22] The report cites two enormous challenges for the student engaged in formation for ministry. First, the explosion of knowledge, pluralism, and consumerism and a host of other complicating factors make huge demands on what a minister must know to be effective in ministry. Second, with the erosion of thick religious subcultures, the novice minister has fewer sources of practical wisdom to draw upon. The Alban report notes, "The communities of practice that their predecessors could count on have disappeared. Increasingly, [new] pastors are on their own."[23]

Fortunately, the study went on to draw a number of heartening conclusions. Among them are three that should encourage you in your work.

- Students value what you have to offer and say so. One participant reports: "I feel like I've learned so much through conversations with [my pastoral mentors] as well as by watching them 'in action.' I appreciate their willingness to share their own ministry experiences or even the thinking behind decisions they've made. I'm constantly learning in ministry—learning about myself, the congregation, God and the community."[24]
- Seasoned pastors have something important to teach new clergy. Further, when they are given opportunities to teach new pastors, profoundly valuable knowledge becomes available to the church.
- People are formed for ministry not just in classrooms but also by practicing the work—and reflecting on it—with others (especially working ministers like you).[25]

These conclusions will certainly not surprise you. In fact, the very formation the study supports is championed by field educators and underscored by practical theologian John Paver, formerly of the Uniting Church Theological College in Melbourne, Australia, when he writes, "My central belief [is] that theory and practice must critically have a dialogue with and inform each other in order that theological education becomes a unified rather than a fragmented enterprise."²⁶ In other words, your work with the student, doing and reflecting on ministry practice together, provides the bridging experience between classroom and the world of ministry.

The importance of your role in this partnership cannot be overstated. The next generation of ministers, if they are to be more fully formed for ministry, depends on it. But not supervisor-mentors exclusively. Thank heaven that the God who calls is also the God who forms for ministry. This knowledge, like the word that came to the prophet Jeremiah—"Before I formed you in the womb I knew you, and before you were born I consecrated you" (Jer. 1:5)—has encouraged and sustained prophets, apostles, priests, and pastors to this day. This is the grace and mystery of call.

Your significant role in this formation for ministry commitment also retains an element of mystery. Michael Pollan, in *The Botany of Desire*, provides an apt illustration. Slice an apple in half at its equator and you will find five small chambers arrayed in a perfectly symmetrical starburst—a pentagram. Each chamber holds a seed or two. Imagine that the apple is a Honey Crisp. Should you plant the seeds, each would result in a completely new and different apple—and none of them a Honey Crisp!²⁷ Each of the students that we as field education faculty and you as supervisor-mentor are privileged to work with become, by the grace of God, the minister that God intends for them to be, each one uniquely fitted for kingdom service. This is the mystery and grace of supervision and mentoring in field education—as well as its freedom.

On behalf of all field educators, thank you for being our colleague.

2
The Art of Supervision and Formation

CHARLENE JIN LEE

A new subject can seem more graspable when it is presented in precise bullet points than when it is subtly described in poetry. Most of us like certainty more than possibilities, answers more than questions. We want to know how to do something, and we want to learn it step by step—and quickly. We seek efficiently packaged information and sound bites just interesting enough to capture our fleeting attentions. Yet, most of us who engage the realm of the mysteries of life, beauty, pain, and death—namely, ministry—know too well that neither a dictionary of terms nor a manual of procedures is sufficient for substantively describing the dance of discerning and living faithfully into one's call.

Rather than following a prescribed linear progression, being and becoming a minister entails gliding, stumbling, circling, dipping—swirling in and out of hope and despair, struggling between belief and doubt, living in the borderlands of an unyielding faith and a desperation to rediscover truth. This being and becoming cannot be neatly explained or taught with systematic guidelines. The complex process of formation requires a language that allows space for unsystematic yet authentic representations of experience.

What you will not find in this chapter is a methodology for supervision or an outlined program for facilitating the formation of interns. What you are invited to consider, however, is a way of being and becoming that recognizes the mystery and reverence of the task with which you are entrusted as a supervisor-mentor. The chapter is an invitation to consider an aesthetic approach to the forms and moments of life in ministry. It is an invitation to consider ministry supervision as one might engage works of art: with a posture of receptivity.

A Poetics of Ministry

Poetry, a communication that attends to and nuances the affective, aesthetics, forms and meanings of the concrete, provides a helpful heuristic lens for observing the contours of ministry, just as it helps ministers consider the responsibility of supervising the formation of others in ministry.

Creative freedom and intentional restraint are found in the artful strokes of a poet. Both spontaneous effect and deliberate technique are at work in composition. This process also includes being prepared for the dawning of new contours between an initial vision and the finished form. The final form, in actuality, is *un*finished, because its words carry on beyond the author, weaving in and out of the interpretations drawn by those who experience the composition in different places and times.

Artful supervision looks something like this. You bring your unique perspectives and wisdom to the formation of an intern. Yet, these will converge with the particular histories and gifts an intern brings. At times you will provide an intern with theological rationales and hermeneutical groundings for the sermon you have preached the past week. More often an intern will simply experience your preaching voice and be shaped by what she gleans from the experience itself. At times, an intern will need your feedback and even correction. At other times, an intern will simply need some space to try things out without the fear of hearing from you, "What *I* would have done is . . ."

The interaction between supervisor and intern is a sacred one because of its creative and relational dimensions. Creation is at work in every engagement of learning: something new is formed, or something that always was is re-formed. The following haiku conveys the constructive activity of teaching and the experience of formation that a supervisor-mentor and intern encounter together during an internship year:

We meet awkwardly.
I invite you to walk.
I find you dancing.[1]

Two individuals meet. In that meeting, a congregation is also introduced. As they begin their work together, unfamiliarity with one another's sensibilities or "the surprise of the recognizable self" in the other, that is, a glimpse of yourself in another, a connection, marks the beginning of the shared work.[2] Each enters the work with ideas, expectations, and motivations that sometimes overlap but often differ from the other person's. What is certain is that, by the final day of the internship, initial visions of the internship arrangement will have been challenged, reshaped, and revisioned. Much is received and given along the way. Most of what is learned and taught is not quantifiable. Articulating the content of this interaction is often difficult because formation relies less on content and more on the context of the learning: the relationship.

Relational Formation

Walking together is a useful poetic image to transpose to the art of supervision. I teach a class on transformational pedagogy in which I ask students to propose metaphors for the ministry of teaching. One student brought a rustic wooden walking stick to class and explained that the minister is like a walking stick as she supports alongside and helps balance the one who is walking. The walking stick does not go ahead. It stays beside, sometimes behind. It absorbs the walker's weight when needed and serves as a physical symbol of support for the one walking, who gains more confidence just knowing that the stick is there.

Similarly, an invitation to walk is an invitation to walk *with*. In many African cultures, a parent will often call a growing child to go on a walk. They have no destination or an agenda. Sometimes they talk, sometimes they are silent. Always, the relationship is reinforced. The child grows by knowing he is loved and through understanding the ways of his father. A parent's attentive care isn't literally verbalized: it is experienced, then known. This walking together is an intimate activity.

Applying these images of walking together and the metaphor of a walking stick to the relationship between the supervisor-mentor and the intern, one can see that the supervisor-mentor has a posture of receptivity in the relationship. The interaction between a supervisor and an intern is open and mutually dependent. The supervisor relinquishes control while remaining ready to "see what is there and let what is there speak."[3] While some people might think the lack of control reflects passivity, to stay beside and sometimes slightly behind a student takes great strength and self-understanding.

A walking stick serves quietly, but it must be strong. A supervisor embodies the strength of gentleness and restraint when carefully attending to an intern as he takes strides, helping when he stumbles and remaining in the background as he finds his own strength and self-understanding. Lao Tzu, father of Taoism, offers wisdom for understanding this kind of leadership posture: "A leader is best when people barely know she exists, not so good when people obey and acclaim her. A good leader talks little when her work is done. When her aim is fulfilled, they will say: We did it ourselves."[4] Therefore, the student who is found dancing has not learned the intricacies of the steps from his teacher. Rather, the teacher created a welcoming space in which the student could join the teacher in the dance. Over time, from the hospitality and freedom of the space, new ideas and new movements emerge—expressions that surpass the original vision.

Embodied Supervision

Conventional understanding is that a supervisor oversees performance, manages operations, and directs others to carry out delegated tasks. These perfunctory roles create a relational distance between the supervisor and the supervised. A picture of a supervisor walking across a factory floor with a clipboard comes to mind. She is making rounds to be sure that people are doing their jobs. Typically, a supervisor is understood more by her functions (what she does) than by her person (who she is).

A supervisor of a ministerial intern must be understood more by her person than by her functions. It is impossible to separate the roles of a minister from who the minister is. Likewise, it is impossible to lead others in discerning a vocation in ministry without having contemplated and continuing to contemplate one's own sense of call. There is, then, very little distance between a teacher and a student, between a supervisor and an intern, and between one's responsibilities as a supervisor and one's responsibilities as a minister.

A supervising pastor supervises by the very act of ministering. He does not put on the supervisory hat when he sits with an intern for weekly meetings or when he observes an intern making her first pastoral care visit or preaching her first sermon. The supervisory role is not fulfilled when a supervisor completes evaluation forms or explains to the intern the life of a particular congregation and the pastoral duties in it. Rather, active supervision takes place when a supervising pastor engages in ministry: when she leads worship, meditates on Scripture, prays for congregants, moderates meetings, celebrates communion, teaches young people, visits the sick, greets worshipers, comforts the mourning, expresses appreciation for the office staff, and keeps sabbath. All of these ministry acts are vital parts of supervision. Supervision is more than modeling, however; it is living. How the supervising pastor lives offers substantive glimpses for an intern who is seeking not only to know the how-to of ministry but more so to understand life in ministry.

Educators and supervisor-mentors alike often mistakenly think people are interested in the information we can offer them. In the case of technical training, this may be true. But when formation is involved, people are much more interested in who we are than in what we do. I experienced the distinctions between technical training and formational learning as a piano student.

For one year before beginning grammar school, my parents sent me to a piano conservatory every day. The first words I learned to read and write were terms from music theory. I practiced running my fingers through Hanon's scale exercises and checked off the boxes the teacher had drawn to indicate the number of times I was to practice the exercises. During lessons, the teacher would sit on a chair at one end of the piano and watch me. Many hours of my childhood were spent on the piano bench, often with a metronome ticking above, where I learned the techniques of maneuvering my fingers according to the printed music notes. Obediently following the dizzying array of black dots on paper, I matriculated over time from beginning level books to more technically challenging pieces.

Many years later I realized that the formation of a piano virtuoso was about far more than training. One teacher, instead of simply watching me practice, allowed me to watch her practice. Before I learned a new piece, she would bring her own copy of the music, which was full of penciled notations, the edges of the sheets rolled and frayed. She would sit at the center of the piano bench and begin to play the piece. Sometimes her eyes were closed as if she were in a dream, sometimes her eyes focused intensely at the measures of the printed music. Her body would sway as if to dance, and her face expressed something inward she could not hide. I watched my teacher interact with the text of the music; she would then watch as I tried out my own interactions with the text. I discovered and rediscovered that the activity of pressing wooden keys with my fingers was more than merely this. It was remembering the composition, creating sound, and evoking interpretation.

While good technique is valuable, ministry is about more than skills. Indeed, acquiring and practicing the skills of active listening, critical exegesis, public speaking, and effective administration is important for a pastor. As supervisors, we are eager to teach those preparing for pastoral vocations to do these tasks properly and well; we want to ensure that an intern has every opportunity to observe and practice skills such as preaching, assisting with wedding and funeral planning, leading a Bible study for youth, following along on three hospital pastoral care visits, observing a session or board meeting. And so the intern completes the items on the list, . . . check, check, check. However, if doing all of these tasks ensured one's readiness for a lifelong vocation in ministry, then they ought to be analyzed and a formula generated to guarantee ministerial effectiveness.

The classical training I received on the piano followed a regimen established long before I sat at the piano bench for the first time. An effective and efficient method for teaching the correct conditioning of hands and fingers was already in place. So that students would acquire the necessary technical skills in a cumulative progression, pieces requiring certain techniques were introduced in a particular order. Such a formula tested over time is appealing because it has a proven record of meeting set objectives. There is safety in adhering to a formula for teaching and learning because it presupposes that outcomes are reproducible. Indeed, in room after room at the conservatory, students diligently and impressively moved their fingers through very difficult musical compositions.

Formation is different from training, however. Formation presupposes that an outcome cannot be known in advance because an individual's experience in the formation process, not the process itself, is at the center. In addition, relying on sets of lessons is ineffective for formation because its "curriculum" is created organically as it is lived. The course for formation is actively composed by the explicative activity of individuals, their interactions with others.

While training can be likened to adherence to an instructions manual, ministerial formation through an internship is like injecting poetry into a structured program. This form of learning and becoming is fluid. Poetic forms are movements that inject disorder and unpredictability into a program concerned only with reproduction.

In the risky yet creative space of a course open for exploration is an opportunity for every student to authenticate his identity, speak with her own voice, and interpret the forms and meanings of ministry through his own contextual reality.

As a student experiences the course of learning typical of a formational internship, dialogue that both complicates and illuminates the learning process arises. This dialogue contains questions, ponderings, imaginations, hopes, and fears now named and considered. Such dialogue often leads to incomplete and awkward understanding, yet is necessary for education that is formational: this learning invites a student to explore self-identity and to contemplate self in ministry. The dialogue, then, is the authentic interaction between the learner and the learning experience. Madeline Grumet, professor of education at the University of North Carolina, writes, "Education emerges as a metaphor for a person's dialogue with the world of his or her experience. . . . To delete dialogue from this experience would be to relegate learning to a series of reactive, conditioned behaviors best described as training."[5]

Perhaps what is needful for supervision is space for dialogue, for interaction; space where not everything is explained, told, corrected, and taught; space where dialogue—both shared publicly and reflected on privately—is encouraged and sustained.

As One Being Taught

The natural question that follows, then, is how does a supervisor encourage and sustain dialogue? What must a supervisor do and not do so that the internship is formational rather than training-oriented? What techniques create a welcome space for questions? How does a supervisor maintain a receptive disposition when a student is impatient to receive a supply of answers? The response to these good questions about methods remains nonmethodological; rather than delineating a set of techniques, what follows is a consideration of a *posture* of being and becoming.

I will return to my experience as a student of classical piano. Watching my teacher practice awakened me to the exquisite complexities of music. When she played, it was as if I was not there, as if she had forgotten that she was supposed to teach me. She was simply practicing her art. The many handwritten notations on the sheets of music told me that careful thought and intention were behind her playing. Occasionally, she would miss a note. She would sometimes stop to correct herself but she did not stop to apologize or explain to me why she made the mistake. She was learning each time she played. She was not afraid to show the learner in her. She was not, after all, a perfect master of technique. She was one who danced with the text of the music as if having complicated conversation; I witnessed this conversation. Eventually, I would emulate this "danceful" conversation, except with my own discovered forms and intentions, following my own notations on what would become my own frayed and thin sheets of music.

Supervision that encourages and sustains dialogue for exploration and discovery also recognizes that the supervising pastor is also and always in formation. Formation is ongoing for all of us who discern our place in the mystery of the infinite God who would choose to incarnate holy love and compassion through our humanness. For those who understand God's radical act of incarnate ministry, faithfully living into one's vocation means seeking new meanings and reminders of one's identity in the scope of God's activity in the world.

Indeed, a supervisor-mentor is being and becoming, formed and being formed. One does not ultimately arrive or finish the course of formation after a certain number of years in ministry. While a pastor who has walked through many seasons in ministry may have learned skills for handling issues that at an earlier time seemed much larger than they do in retrospect, years of ministry experience ought to cultivate a posture of humility, not a mastery of skills. Humility is a mark of wisdom, a better understanding of our true selves, and a capacity to see ourselves as we really are. We often mistake our acquired abilities to speak eloquently in public, expound on theological concepts, plan and lead creative liturgy, offer prayers that evoke emotions, and so forth as marks of a good pastor who is ready and able to supervise others who want to become good pastors.

When ministers adopt a posture of humility, they recognize that their capacity for ministry depends on their receptivity to continuous formation. They also recognize that they do not and cannot fully know or substantially explain the vastness of God. Humility is cultivated when we recognize the "unfinishedness"[6] of our knowing and being. It is cultivated when we grapple with the humanness of our inward being and the divine call of God upon our life. By authentically engaging this dialogue about our human limitations and simultaneous propensity for living into a holy vocation, a supervising pastor creates space for others to contemplate, explore, discover, and release their own expressions of being and becoming.

This dialogue shuts down quickly when a supervisor satisfies the impatient need—and desire—to provide clear-cut explanations, to supply pat answers, and to present only a posture of confidence and clarity about what it means to stand with and for God in the gap between brokenness and redemption. When a supervisor invites others to observe and join the ongoing dialogue with which she herself is engaged, she shapes the formation of interns who will likewise grow in humility and wisdom.

In biblical Hebrew, the words for "to teach" and "to learn" share the same consonantal root. This root is used in a description of leadership found in Isaiah 50: "The Lord God has given me the tongue of a teacher, that I may know how to sustain the weary with a word. Morning by morning he wakens—wakens my ear to listen as those who are taught" (v. 4). The Hebrew word for "teacher" translated in English is limmudim: למודים *Limmudim* literally means "those who are taught." The same word is used in Isa. 8:16 to refer to Isaiah's disciples. In Hebraic understanding, the teacher is essentially a learner. The writer of this text is describing how God is teaching him to minister, giving him words to speak and forming him to stand with those who are weak. The responsibility of the prophet to lead others is beyond his expertise. He can only lead as he is being taught. He can only teach as one who is receiving knowledge. The reception of knowledge does not grow progressively to reach a point where one has full understanding. Growing as a teacher requires ongoing receptivity to being taught.

One who leads others must be taught daily, "morning by morning." This idea blurs the boundary between teaching and learning that conventional North American understandings of education demarcate. Our understanding of the teacher as a subject-matter expert or as the keeper of knowledge awaiting transmission is different from the disposition of the teacher as humble and wise, as portrayed in the Isaiah text. The biblical translators, I imagine, had to make a contextual hermeneutical jump and place *teacher* (instead of *learner*) where *limmudim* is used in the original language.

As one who supervises others in formation, the internship supervisor must recognize that he is in need of formation, too. Formation is a necessary activity for all who are responding to God's call: both the one who has just recognized the call and the one who has been discerning the shape and meaning of that call daily for perhaps thirty years or more.

As One Writing Letters

A Buddhist teaching describes three ways of being in the world: like letters carved on a rock, traced in sand, written on running water.[7] Mary Doll, a curriculum theorist, draws from this teaching to describe phenomenological pedagogy (study that attends to one's experienced perception of the learning structure and its process).[8] I have found this Buddhist teaching and Doll's use of these insightful metaphors helpful for imaging the art of ministry supervision.

Training is like carving procedures onto a rock. There is something didactic, rigid, and even forceful in such a metaphor. Engraving on a hard surface infers permanence. Knowledge that is permanently carved assumes its objective and universal nature; knowledge that is unchangeable presumes certain information as more useful and applicable to all contexts. A training handbook on how to do ministry is helpful only when *information* is desired. When *formation* is desired, and necessary, offering training—disseminating information as if carving it onto a rock—is inadequate, because such ways of teaching ignore the creative and relational dimension of transformational learning experiences.

By contrast, writing letters on running water is an apt metaphor for transformational teaching and learning. There is fluidity, movement, and even uncertainty in this image. The moment the ink touches the water, it seems to disappear. Yet, while the diluted ink cannot be seen, the writing, though momentary, does inject change. The water's composition and nature are changed by the ink.

The kind of learning experience a supervising minister extends is determined by how she images the intern student. A rock is solid, stationary, formed. Its contours are defined. Running water is always forming. It has been somewhere and it is going somewhere. Sometimes it flutters by, sometimes it moves formidably. Water flows through shallow brooks and reaches deep crevices. Its contours are not bound.

A supervising minister who images the intern student as running water understands that she plays a supportive role in the Creator's ministry of formation and transformation. Something is already happening to and around the intern and minister even before they knowingly enter into the learning situation. Even before a person enters a classroom or steps into a church or receives the preached word, formation has begun. And formation will continue to be authored by our Creator and Caller. With such an understanding, a supervisor has little anxiety about giving a conclusive report or assessment of an intern's readiness to face the challenges of life in ministry. The supervisor is less preoccupied about teaching correct methods and more intentional about living faithfully into the call of ministry.

Viewing supervision as writing letters on already forming interns is a freeing and humble approach. The supervisor does not have information, answers, and explanations to impart. Rather, the supervisor writes a letter simply as a faithful witness to compassion clothing brokenness, mercy restoring unfinishedness, Holy God calling foolishness. The apostle Paul describes the Christian testimony this way: "You yourselves are our letter, written on our hearts, to be known and read by all; and you show that you are a letter of Christ, prepared by us, written not with ink but with the Spirit of the living

God, not on tablets of stone but on tablets of human hearts" (2 Cor. 3:2). It seems as if Paul and Buddha are having a conversation about how one might faithfully live in the world with others. Our very lives are letters written to others. The letters we write describe the daily transformations that enable ordinary people to offer life-giving words to the weary, to ordain blessing upon the meek, to extend hands of healing upon the weak, to prophesy radical hope of shalom in a world made lopsided by greed—not that we have become expert in these acts of ministry, but because we are recipients of them. For we too are like running water on which letters are written by those who teach us and by the One who teaches us.

Supervision as Conversation

A poetical description of ministerial supervision and formation recognizes the art of being attentive to the realm of the divine while living in the seeming flatness of the ordinary. It recognizes the palpable middle space between lucid theology and the unknownness of God, between answers and question. It recognizes the quiet discernment necessary to know when to speak and when to listen, when to act and when to remain in reflection. It recognizes the unfinishedness of each one's participation in the grand movement of God in this world. It also recognizes the need for pastors and pastors-to-be to cultivate capacities for ministry that express thoughtful practice.

This description of the nature of ministry informs an approach to internship supervision that requires artistry for sustaining dialogue: an approach to supervision that creates space to *stay* with possibilities, permission to *be* without the preoccupation to arrive somewhere by a certain time in a certain form. It requires complicated conversations.

So we enter into a complicated conversation about faithfully living into one's ministry even as we "supervise" those who urgently look to us to supply them with information and eagerly seek to obtain clarity about the meaning of ministry and a vocation in it. In the midst of conversations complicated by dialogue rather than simplified by answers, what we soon find is that inviting others to walk with us as we navigate between unspeakable joy and undeniable helplessness creates space for authentic conversations about the shape of faithful ministry, not about the procedures for successful ministry.

A crucial part of this complicated conversation is our willingness to present ourselves as learners who continue to seek understanding and discovery. The teacher who is unsatisfied with flighty answers to deep questions participates in the formation of a student who will contemplate the questions of ultimate meaning. The teacher who perceives the unknownness of God participates in the formation of a student who stands before truth with reverence. The teacher who creates space for others to interact with the living text of the Divine participates in the formation of a student who extends hospitality to the spiritually homeless so prevalent in our midst.

3
Ministerial Reflection

EMILY CLICK

Field education helps you the student build habits of ministerial reflection. These reflective practices make you more effective in leading faith communities. Ministers who build patterns of contemplation learn to listen carefully to the words expressed by congregants during significant ministerial moments. Yet you also will find that ministerial observation goes far beyond listening to words. As you build habits of reflection, you will become more attuned to the multiple meanings embedded in situations and to the layers of interpretation you might make about an incident. Field education works to develop more than habits of meditation; its goal is to enable you to integrate multiple types of reflection into a coherent framework. That integrative process enables you to form an interpretation so that you can help congregations act upon their deepest callings from the gospel. Then you will learn, after acting, to reflect again on what you have done, to consider next steps toward faithful ministry.

Ministers build bridges between their congregants' lives and their own ministry practices such as preaching and teaching. Therefore, ask yourself, "How do I relate to others and bring my story, my own experiences, into these relationships in appropriate ways?" You also will ask, "Where is God in the midst of our lives, or how do

I interpret God's apparent absence?" These questions animate the heart of ministerial reflection. You will learn how to think about the actions you and others take and how to interpret those actions in light of theological principles. You also will interpret your actions in relation to other theories, such as psychological ones or ethical principles. This reflection on action will enable you to act even more faithfully as you go forward.

In the mid-1980s, the highly influential researcher of professional development and MIT professor Donald Schön wrote an influential pair of texts that explored the role of reflection in developing professional effectiveness.[1] These texts showed the ways professionals must learn to reflect while in the midst of their work and also after completing professional tasks. Schön demonstrated that educating what he called reflective practitioners needed a specific mentoring approach. This approach is designed to enable students to build habits of knowing what they know and how they know it. In other words, contemplation is crucial to effective professional functioning because it surfaces foundational assumptions and interpretations. Yet, practitioners do not just reflect on other people's lives. Inevitably, we also bring our own lives into these reflections. The art of ministerial reflection therefore calls for us to know who we are, who others are, and how God is at work in the many ways our lives are intertwined.

Ministerial reflection might at first appear to be an extravagant way to spend time, like the weekend at a spa far removed from the important work to which you are called. It would be understandable if you were to perceive ministerial reflection as a time-out from the real work of ministry, such as visiting those in prison or writing a liturgical prayer. Instead, however, ministerial reflection is the crucial key to all of the work of ministry. For only through careful consideration can you put together pieces that otherwise seem disjointed, irrelevant, or confusing. Reflection enables you to weave the integrative thread that you then will offer to the community as its members weave the tapestry of God's missional purpose in its midst.

Consider Rachel's experience in her field education congregation. While the minister and Rachel's supervisor, Cassandra, is out of town, a beloved two-year-old child of key members in the church dies, tragically, by drowning in the backyard pool. The minister will return from her out-of-town trip as soon as possible to do this funeral, with Rachel assisting her along the way. But in the meantime, Rachel goes to visit the family in their grief. Here are some of her reflections as she drives back to the church after her meeting with the family in their home:

> I wonder if I said the right things to them, or at least did not harm them with what I said. I never knew that Charles and Susanna's marriage was about to fail, and now it seems unlikely to survive, especially since Susanna blames Charles's drinking for his neglect of their daughter. Is it really his fault? Is his drinking bad enough that he might harm other family members? How will this death and their failing marriage affect the deacons' retreat next month, since Charles is on the deacons' committee? Does anyone else know about his drinking? And what about their older child, Stephen? He was awfully silent during our time together. What's going on there? He reminds me of my brother and how he used to close up when our family started to argue.

Rachel will reflect many times on that situation throughout her time in field education. Her ruminations about the situation will prove crucial to her formation as an effective minister and will influence her theological perspective, her capacity to engage in difficult situations, and her compassion for the people with whom she engages ministry. Her reflections will take place as an inner conversation, with her supervisor for field education, and, hopefully, in the context of peer conversations and in several classroom settings. These considerations help her develop her capacity for counseling, funeral planning, and prayerful intervention in a troubled family situation.

Field education, at its best, will teach Rachel a number of skills such as those listed above. Certainly, she needs to learn how to talk with people who are grieving and how to inform such a conversation with the resources of faith. She will also learn how to do a funeral for a grief-filled family and community that attends to their broken hearts and their faith-related questions. The central purpose of field education is to remind Rachel that she must pay attention to something beyond the tasks related to this ministerial situation. She also must learn to slow down her thinking process while on that drive home and capture the multiple layers of reflection she needs to engage to fully understand and interpret what is happening in the many lives affected by this tragic turn of events. And she must learn that one of those lives affected is her own.

Rachel needs to explore many things to fully understand what is happening in this moment of ministry. Why is her leading concern during her inner conversation on the drive home about what she says or does not say? What does that tell her about herself and her assumptions about what would and would not be helpful in any situation? Next, she may want to consider how much she knows about marital stress and how these types of major life incidents can affect marital relationships. She also might want to learn what she can about alcoholism and its effects on family dynamics. If she truly suspects that Charles's drinking may be putting remaining family members at risk, she may have legal responsibility to follow through on those suspicions.

In addition to these types of deliberations, Rachel will want to think about the church as an organization, including events like deacons' retreats and meetings, and how these too are affected by significant life upsets such as the tragic death of a child or the untreated alcoholism of a committee member. She will want to begin thinking about how the core teachings of her church about God's presence in times of loss will best be upheld in the days ahead. She will want to think about the faith questions that will arise, including whether or not this was God's plan or judgment, or whether it is "just a twist of fate." She needs to listen to all sorts of interpretations that members of the congregation will offer for what has happened and interpret the situation from a theological point of view. Finally, she may want to reflect on the challenge of thinking about her own family while being engaged in ministry to another family. She will want to learn how to ponder the assumptions she makes about other families because of the dynamics at work in her own.

Many students today come to seminaries and divinity schools during their third decade of life. Some are keenly aware of their own limited life experience. So when they encounter a situation like the one Rachel suddenly finds herself in, they can wonder, what do I have to offer? It might even be the first time they have actually experienced the death of someone they know. Ministerial reflection can serve to boost a student's ability to function outside of comfort zones with a degree of appropriate confidence that he or she can indeed offer something of real value to those in need. Reflective ministers bring more than skills to situations; they also bring a capacity to help individuals in challenging situations build perspectives that integrate and honor their faith. While ministers build this capacity over the entire span of their professional lives, young and relatively inexperienced ministers can offer just as compassionate and effective care as can those with longer resumes. And they will learn to develop their reflective capacity throughout their professional lives.

Types of Reflection in Ministry

Rachel's story demonstrates that reflection on ministry involves many types of thinking that all go on more or less at the same time. Just as she is thinking how to respond to someone who says this child's death is God's will, she will also experience her inner pain over the loss, her indignation at theological perspectives that differ from her own, and the limits of her own understanding of how God allows good people to suffer. She also will be thinking of logistical concerns, like whether to pick up her robe from the dry cleaner's, whether to arrange childcare for the tentative date for the funeral, and whether she should ask for an extension on the paper due in one of her seminary classes. She may feel more like a juggler than a minister, and handling these multiple types of reflection at once can seem dizzying.

That is why field education builds in several types of deliberation. You will work throughout your field education experience with a supervisor-mentor who has received some training in how to teach new ministers about reflecting in just these types of situations. In addition, in most schools you will enroll in a course designed to help you think in partnership with peers, other students who are enrolled in similar types of situations. Many of these groups reflect together using case studies, which is the subject of another chapter in this book. Each of these venues is designed specifically to help you develop your own way of meditating on ministerial experiences so that you can build muscles for a lifetime of interpreting situations.

Supervisor-mentors guide you to develop your own artistry for ministry. I use this term *artistry* advisedly. Your own way of practicing what Gregory the Great called the "art of arts," or ministry, will be unique to you. Your supervisor will want you to develop the particular gifts God has given you and to employ those in ways that enhance the whole people of God. The supervisor has been chosen because he or she understands that you may preach, teach, and counsel in ways quite different from their ways. And yet, they have also accumulated a great deal of wisdom about how to approach ministerial situations. Your mentor will advise you on best practices, and he or she will trust you to jump into situations and try to do your best. You might think the greatest learning comes from doing: from preaching, reading Scripture, and counseling. In part, you would be right. You may also find, however, that some of your most significant learning develops when you reflect, with your mentor, on some of the issues you failed to notice, or noticed but didn't know what to do with, while you were involved in "doing" ministry.

For example, Rachel may have a supervisory session with Cassandra upon her return. Rachel may ask, "How do you know if you have said the right thing or done harm by saying the wrong thing?" Cassandra might respond in a variety of ways. She may choose to suggest options for what the student might say in these types of situations, including some Scripture passages often used when encountering grieving families. However, Cassandra might instead ask

Rachel to reflect on why she views ministry in these situations as bound up in what is or is not said. Similarly, Cassandra might skip Rachel's presenting question and ask her to reflect on where she saw God present and active in the room while she met with the family.

These are just a few examples of how a supervisor-mentor might stimulate Rachel's development of her reflective capacity. The most artful supervisory session might include several layers of reflection. So, Rachel might, for example, mention how the surviving child reminded her of her own brother. Cassandra might link this observation to an earlier theological assertion made by Rachel, such as "I believe God was in the room mourning with that family." Cassandra might ask about how Rachel's connection with the surviving child might both interfere with and enhance her ministry, how she feels about the connection, what meaning she attaches to it, and how God might honor that connection. In making these types of observations, the supervisor-mentor is not just teaching what to say in these types of situations. Cassandra is also demonstrating for Rachel how one type of reflection can inform and integrate with another.

Ministerial Reflection with Peers

Just as you learn from reflecting with your supervisor-mentor, you also will learn through reflecting with your peers. In many field education programs, you will enroll in coursework that supplements the learning you experience at the ministry site. These courses often call for you to write up records of conversations, known as verbatim, or case studies about ministry incidents that were somewhat confusing to you.

One of the richest offerings of field education resides in the ways it opens you up to experiences you may never otherwise have in ministry. The student, for example, who is studying to be a college chaplain may learn a great deal from hearing Rachel reflect on her experience with Charles and Susanna, the deacons, and the children. These experiences have much in common with but are also distinct from those of a college chaplain. The student who is doing field education as a college chaplain, through reflecting with Rachel, will learn how to engage with congregations facing tragic loss. As they reflect together, they will assist each other in making sense of the many threads weaving throughout the case.

Peer reflective groups help you in another way as well. While it can be reassuring and instructive to work with someone who has been in ministry for many years, sometimes only those who are new to the journey can fully identify with the questions and confusions you are experiencing. For example, one student might share with his peer group that his supervisor-mentor requested he dress in a more professional manner. Only other students will immediately be able to understand the confusion over what that means, as well as the obvious problem of how to pull off more professional dress on a limited student budget and so forth. Since they are figuring out precisely the same issues, they can be a most valuable resource.

Yet, peer reflective groups can also present problems, just as you can encounter challenges in the supervisory relationship. Supervisors or peers can reinforce problematic assumptions. You can imagine a peer group joining in to discredit the supervisor-mentor who asks the student to dress professionally as out of touch with the realities of student budgets and priorities. Supervisors may provide standardized answers rather than allow you to find your own way. When supervisors or peers reinforce your own defensiveness, you may need to work harder to face your own challenges and make difficult but necessary adjustments. Yet on the other hand, you are more likely to recognize your need to face parts of yourself you resist reflecting upon if your peers or supervisor help you see the importance of doing so. You will need to balance the input of peers with the teachings of your supervisor-mentor. And you will need to reflect in prayerful ways about what God is teaching you in every situation.

One other aspect of peer reflective groups is especially worthy of notice. Whether you attend a denomination-related seminary or one that requires all students and faculty to sign a faith affirmation or a divinity school with multiple faith traditions, you will encounter diverse theological perspectives among your colleagues. Some will want to label your theological stance, whatever it is, problematic or possibly even toxic. Others will find it interesting, although different from their own. Other students may share precisely your same theological point of view. These matters can become quite challenging when it comes to integrating faith perspectives with real-life issues such as the death Rachel encountered in her field education setting.

For example, Rachel might present her encounter with the family right after the death as a case at her peer reflective seminar. She writes up the way she talked with the family and how they responded. She includes her observation of Stephen's isolation and her concerns about the marriage. And she concludes her write-up with this statement: "I wanted them to come to understand that Jesus has a plan for their lives, and that although mysterious, Jesus even had a plan for how this death would change their lives and all of our lives."

Rachel may discover that many Christians differ on how they view wording about God or Jesus having a "plan." This makes it inevitable, in any theological school, that some students would resonate with Rachel's interpretation of a death and others would find it problematic. To have a full discussion of such a case, it will become necessary for students to express something of their own point of view on this issue. It would likely be inauthentic for those with differing views to simply pretend to affirm Rachel's interpretation. Rachel will probably learn that hearing other perspectives will help her to clarify and strengthen her own stance. The best peer reflective groups learn how to build respect for their differing points of view on a situation.

Peer reflective groups are of value, for if they are expertly facilitated, ministers in formation grow to appreciate the distinctive qualities of their own theological stance. They are enabled to see the strengths and weaknesses of their own approach. They can see how someone they know well, and hopefully respect, can listen carefully and yet emerge with a deeply contrasting point of view about how God cares for humanity even in the midst of tragedy. These types of differing points of view are of value theologically; they are also of value in forming a professional capacity for operating as ministers within groups that disagree. Developing a capacity for fulsome appreciation of different points of view is of vital importance for ministers. The strongest leaders know how to work in groups with diverse perspectives on how to address important problems.

These two types of reflection, with an expert guide and with peers, help you to develop tools for future ministry. You will most often have some kind of relationship with peers with whom you reflect upon your ministries. Similarly, you will want to keep in touch with spiritual directors, mentors, or other guides as you sort through your growing understanding of God's call in your life. In other words, field education helps you learn how to build the kinds of sustaining relationships you will need throughout your ministry. These structural supports for reflection are not just for the formational, early stage but also integral components to the reflective life of the pastoral professional. The problems you may experience in either type of relationship, with peers or with supervisors, are just the sort of problems you will experience throughout your life in ministry.

Building the Practice of Integrating Reflections

Field education will help Rachel learn to integrate several types of reflection. One way of describing this is that field education students learn to look at the ways each ministerial situation contains layers of meaning that ministers must consider at the same time, in order to decide how to speak and act faithfully. In Rachel's situation with the family, one aspect of the incident has overwhelming intensity and tragic impact: the terrible loss of the child. But it turns out there is even more to the situation, as Rachel discovers in her caring conversation. It appears that in this home the child may have been neglected in many ways, and there might have existed a pattern that resulted in the accidental death. Furthermore, there is evidence that the home has been marked by tension, symbolized in the way the wife intensifies her own grief and that of others by blaming her husband. Rachel observes the family is maintaining an outward appearance of harmony while the marriage is crumbling. Then there is the surviving child's experience and his way of reacting through withdrawal. Rachel needs to let each feature of the ministerial situation inform the others. She must develop a discipline that ensures that her words, actions, and interpretations are coherent with all of the significant aspects of this situation.

For example, it might not be helpful for Rachel to declare, "This is just a freak accident," because it draws too much of an interpretation in advance of adequate information and does not consult various relevant sources about what happened. The psychological reflections she has engaged in show her that the marriage is at risk, and its outcome may partly hinge on what interpretation they place upon this tragic death. Naming this as a freak accident may occlude the relevance of the father's possible neglect and potential guilt. Rachel does not yet know what happened, and through reflecting, she realizes that she should take care in how she interprets the cause of this death. Her concern over what to say is an emerging instinct that there are, in fact, some things she ought to take care not to say here, and there might be things it would be very helpful to name. Her focus on this may be a sign that she is developing the ministerial instinct that what a minister declares in the initial stages of a grief-filled situation will shape meanings for a long time forward.

Similarly, Rachel needs to reflect upon the family as a system. The surviving child already is functioning as if he has some survivor guilt, and his needs may be overlooked. As she drives home, she may start to plan how Stephen will be included in the funeral ritual and at the burial. She is developing instincts that including him will not just be significant to the health of his faith; it also may serve his psychological healing. How she interacts with Stephen may help the family system come to terms with its new shape, and its now long-term task of grieving, so that they can help each other.

When Rachel plans how she might include Stephen in the funeral service, she lets two different considerations inform each other. She has noticed the psychological pain of Stephen, and she lets this inform how she and her pastor will plan the funeral and burial service. A particular joy of pastoral ministry is that leaders can build rituals that enable healing of multiple kinds of issues, such as Stephen's possibly troubled relationship to his family. Ministerial reflection on psychological, legal, sociological, and cultural issues informs the thoughtful planning of liturgical celebrations, rituals, and proclamations of the word.

Rachel and supervisor-mentor will want to integrate the layers of meaning and see how they inform each other. They will, for example, want to think organizationally: How will the church be present to the family? What will be the deacons' role? What are the logistical considerations about room arrangements, expenses, and so forth in relationship to the upcoming funeral? Does anything need to be rescheduled? They will also want to think pastorally. Who will notice the needs of the surviving child? Who else in the community has lost children, and how will they be affected by this tragedy? Who will name the complicating reality of the husband's alcoholism? What can be done to address the anguish of all in this family? Finally, she will want to think theologically. The family, the pastoral staff, and the whole community will be asking, "Who is God to this family right now?" Is God their comforter? A judge? A punisher? They will want to engage the stories of faith to shape their interpretation of events so that their faith can become resilient enough to survive this initial shock and the challenges that lie ahead.

One way, therefore, to describe ministerial reflection is that it combines organizational, pastoral, and theological reflections into consistent meaning making. Theological statements should ring true to what people are experiencing and help them to know what to do next. Ministers must notice that people may be struggling with troubling aspects of a situation, and their theological interpretations should help them integrate these realities into their faith so that they can move forward with confidence. It also must be said that this type of work, building theological meaning in life situations, is not the sole work of ordained clergy but is the work of the whole people of God. Ministerial reflection is the act of combining information from diverse relevant aspects of a situation into a coherent framework for faithful action.

The main point for you to understand about ministerial reflection is that it is about integrating multiple perspectives so that your faithful actions can be coherent with your foundational beliefs and values. You will want to harmonize the diverse points of view that arise throughout the reflective process. Ministerial reflection is an art in and of itself, for it calls reflective practitioners to pay attention to conflicting, confusing sources of information and to build meaning in the midst of that kind of swampland. Such work is important because it is where the people with whom you share ministry actually live. Life is full of conflict, changing circumstances, and multiple impulses. The work you do in ministerial reflection enables building theologically coherent interpretations of diverse observations about what matters in each situation.

This chapter has introduced the concept of ministerial reflection as a crucial component of field education. Its role is to build ministerial capacities that inform and shape communities as they seek to act upon their faith. Ministerial reflection is something you begin to learn in your community of faith, but field education works hard to strengthen those muscles so that you can pay attention to layers of meaning and how those layers inform each other. Such work is vitally important for those who would engage in the artistry of ministerial leadership.

4
The Use of Case Studies in Field Education

TIM SENSING

Recently, I watched a video about locating and replacing the thermostat on my son's F-150 pickup. As far as auto mechanics is concerned, a thermostat transplant ranks as an easy procedure. Since I had experience replacing brakes, starter motors, and water pumps, I felt I could handle a thermostat. The video, while informative, still left me apprehensive about tearing apart my son's truck. What was the difference between the other repairs and this simple thermostat replacement? My previous experiences with repairs had all involved the helpful guidance of a seasoned technician. This time, as I looked at the engine, I realized I was not ready to fly solo. The video did not supply me with the confidence I needed to take the next step.

As a student minister, you have probably felt the same anxieties about engaging in ministry for the first time, whether it is teaching a class, visiting a hospice patient, serving a meal at a homeless shelter, or leading a meeting. As you approach these intimidating situations, remember that what you will learn from experience will soon become instinct. Take the case of the veteran minister who receives the unexpected news that one of her congregants has just suffered a fatal heart attack. In the midst of an already hectic week, she incorporates pastoral actions that garner congregational resources in order to serve the family in appropriate ways. She coordinates visitations, plans services, organizes others to prepare meals, and supports the family through the crisis. Without consulting a manual, the minister seems to know in her bones where to be, what to say, and whom to call. Through the process, she also covers the routine duties of her ministry. On Sunday night, she finally falls into bed anticipating a good night's rest. An observant bystander might easily be bewildered by the efficient and caring way the minister responded. After the crisis is over, the onlooker might not be able to articulate how the pastor so adeptly managed such a complex situation. The case of the unexpected funeral is worthy of careful examination. Who wants to face their first funeral unprepared?

Funerals rank high on the list of pastoral responsibilities capable of churning the stomach and raising blood pressure. I recall my first funeral, which occurred just months after my arrival at a small church in southern Indiana. The call came from a man who had not attended services in several years. After catching my breath, I met with the family and prepared my homily. When the graveside service concluded, I was approached by a stranger who said, "My sister's name was not Katherine but Kathleen. Everyone who knew her called her 'Kate.'" Twenty-five years later, I still remember the impact of her words. I turned to the left, and I could not locate a textbook. I turned to the right; my mentor lived miles away. I did not have the experience or the wisdom to navigate the storm. I was knee-deep in ministry, and I was unprepared.

Throughout human history, in various trades and guilds, artisans have passed on the skills and wisdom of their professions to able apprentices. Both Testaments are filled with examples that parallel Paul's axiom, "Keep on doing the things that you have learned and received and heard and seen in me, and the God of peace will be with you." (Phil. 4:9). Field education gives you the opportunity to engage the various contexts of ministry. You have the opportunity to put into practice what you have learned in texts, from teachers, and from the faith community so that you too will be competent in your ministry. Apprenticeship, however, is not the only pedagogy your teachers and supervisor-mentors will employ. Another way field educators access the lived experiences of seasoned ministers is through case studies. Case studies introduce you to tasks, dilemmas, and practices of everyday ministry and enhance your confidence for the next time you engage in similar situations.

A short introduction to the theoretical constructs that undergird the case method will enhance your ability to incorporate it into your theological reflection and practice. Cases are learning tools that present stories of actual events and dilemmas faced by real people. Case studies formally examine cases through an assortment of processes common in field education, including ministry reports, verbatims, case histories, and reflections on ethical dilemmas. Utilizing the case method in the classroom or during an internship will enhance your development of analytical, integrative, and decision-making skills and will help you apply what you are learning in other classes. Likewise, they are useful for you to implement in congregational and parachurch settings because they help a diverse group of participants become more creative in addressing community issues. Case studies provide you the opportunity to experience the complexity of ministerial situations in the safety of a classroom. While foreseeing every conceivable contingency is impossible, tapping into the lived experiences of veteran pastors may equip you with greater resources to assimilate and adapt when the unexpected challenge barges into your routine.

Case studies tap into the power of narrative and become a vehicle for understanding lived experiences. Using case studies allows you to impose order on lived experiences, thus making sense of the events, thoughts, and actions in real lives. The experienced minister referred to on the preceding pages who skillfully managed an unexpected funeral had not always known how to respond pastorally to a crisis. She, at one time, stood in your shoes. The first time she assisted with a funeral required her to slow down and observe the senior pastor, make a to-do list, and ask many questions. It took time and experience for her to become the veteran. In due course, her prior knowledge of funerals and her good caring instincts provided her the capacity to offer mercy and grace.

Through case studies, you will explore the ways others come to know and practice their craft in tacit and unmeasurable ways. Exploring someone's story is one way you are able to incorporate expert and local knowledge about pastoral practice into your professional experience. Case studies examine unspoken understanding and translate it into explicit knowledge, allowing it to be integrated with other resources (biblical, historical, and theological).

My field education students have found the case method an invigorating approach to thinking and learning about ministry vicariously through the lives of other students and pastors who have traveled down the same pathways of ministerial formation and ministerial practices. In my courses, I ask students to analyze the lived experiences of others as a way to reflect upon their own professional identity and practice. Furthermore, the case method involves writing a formal case brief, writing original cases from personal experiences, and presenting cases to others.[1]

Analyzing a Case

Field education is all about learning by doing. Likewise, the best way to learn about analyzing a case is to do it. The exercises given throughout this chapter will facilitate your ability to incorporate the case method into your reflective practices.

Good cases emerge from current issues and events. Most cases are not timeless and can quickly lose their relevance. For our purposes in this section, I will use an abbreviated scenario that captures the complexity of most cases, given its significant historical context of September 11, 2001. Most pastors vividly remember their own struggles to find words to say after that fateful day. Some of you might recall the sermon preached by your minister. Throughout the land, some preachers attributed this tragedy to God's revenge on what they deemed to be America's sin. Other sanctuaries remained silent, worship leaders not even acknowledging that the events of

Tuesday before had occurred. Yet, everyone who attended worship the weekend following 9/11 had images of falling towers, dying rescue workers, and rubble and soot burned into their heads. They arrived on Sunday, September 16, 2001, with questions, anger, and confusion. They arrived anticipating hearing a word of hope, a note of consolation, and the gospel of God. The case describing this experience, "No Ordinary Sunday," begs for careful analysis.

> **NO ORDINARY SUNDAY**
>
> Teddy Jackson drove to work on Thursday, September 13, 2001, as he had for the past seventeen years. The events of Tuesday still lingered in his thoughts. Last night's prayer service at the church and then again at the civic center had left him exhausted. Today would be his first day back in the office. The pressing issue before him was what he would preach. Sunday was coming, and he needed time to formulate his thoughts. His mind raced for a moment. What would anyone preach in a time like this? When he arrived at his office, Teddy turned to the lectionary for September 16, Year C. The passages listed included: Jer. 4:11–12, 22–28; Psalm 14; 1 Tim. 1:12–17; and Luke 15:1–10. The task for Thursday lay before him. It was obvious that he would need the rest of the afternoon to sketch out his sermon. Teddy picked up his Bible and began to read 1 Timothy. What could he possibly say that would make any difference?

The dilemma of what to preach on any given Sunday presents itself every week. Ministers throughout the world routinely manage these homiletical decisions. Nevertheless, the case of "No Ordinary Sunday" provides you several different pedagogical avenues to pursue. Depending upon the learning objectives, you could explore the relationship between pastoral care and preaching, the lectionary's role in setting the agenda for the liturgy, hermeneutical approaches for preaching to contemporary issues, among many other options. I often begin a case study by asking my students to identify the most pressing issues that emerge for them. In this case, they often identify the issues of theodicy because the text in Jeremiah seems harsh and contradicts their interpretation of God's role in the terror attacks. Afterward, I ask students to read and reflect upon *The Sunday After Tuesday: College Pulpits Respond to 9/11* by William Willimon, former dean of the chapter at Duke University.[2]

I use the following handout to help students analyze cases. While you will not always use every bulleted item in the handout, allow it to prompt your imagination and critical thinking skills.

HOW TO ANALYZE A CASE

- Analyze the case after reading it through several times:
  1. List the characters and note key details about who they are.
  2. Develop a chronology of events. A timeline places essential facts, events, and developments in a logical order that facilitates keeping the facts straight.
  3. Identify the basic issues (especially those things such as acts, values, or attitudes that influence decisions).
  4. List all the positions that reasonable people might take.
  5. If applicable, create an organization chart that establishes the relationships of people, institutions, or decisions presented in the case.
  6. Include decision(s) and decision maker(s) in your list. Identify the chief players and stakeholders, useful information in a case that calls for a decision, or where a character faces difficult challenges. Also, list other actors and interest groups who have differing information, power, or objectives.
- Analysis about a lived experience will offer an answer to these five questions:
  1. What was done (act)?
  2. When or where was it done (scene)?
  3. Who did it (agent)?
  4. How did he or she do it (agency)?
  5. Why was it done (purpose)?[3]

- Let the facts of the case and the possibilities you have considered ferment in your mind. Mull over the case, think about it casually, and let things flow through your imagination.
- Consider any theoretical material or theological resources (for example, church history or tradition, texts, systematic theology) that would be helpful in clarifying the issues in the case.
- Decide on your course of action. What decision would you likely make given the conditions and information you have available? Be prepared to defend or substantiate your decision. Remember that no decision is without risk.
- Participate in the class discussion by sharing your understanding and insights, your ideas and rationale. Listen to what others see in the case; evaluate their positions. Keep an open mind, and be willing to change it with the presentation of new insights or evidence.

EXERCISE 1

Using the above handout, analyze the case "No Ordinary Sunday."

Simply analyzing a case is insufficient for helping you to move from a novice learner to a seasoned practitioner. Many students will present their analysis to the class or write a case brief as a graded assignment. A necessary step between analyzing a case and presenting one is writing a case brief. Formalizing your analysis will help you garner the full impact of the case method and assist you as you grow in your competence as a pastor. I use the following handout to describe the process of writing a case brief.

HOW TO WRITE A CASE BRIEF
A case brief is a concise document written in response to a specific case.
- Case briefs are short and to the point.
- They focus on a dilemma and describe a decision. Although most dilemmas will have many possible paths, the brief argues for a particular choice.
- Several skills are used in the paper:
    1. The ability to summarize well.

2. The capacity to identify dilemmas and decisions to be made in the case.
3. Sensitivity to the variety of factors that affect the decisions.
4. Application of theology, sociology, ethics, and common sense in a variety of situations.

- Imagine that you are writing a case brief for the members of the class and will be called on to explain your position. Alternative: prepare the brief as a consultant's report to a church board.
- Explore conflicting or contrasting positions on the issue. Put an emphasis on being objective (or identify and then bracket your biases). Think with an open mind, and then decide. After you have thought through the alternatives, pick one position to develop. Do not dismiss other perspectives as not applicable, but concentrate on making your position persuasive.
- Possible outline:
  1. Identify the characters.
  2. Summarize the case.
  3. Identify the problem or issues.
  4. Present the facts and theories that are relevant to the issues.
  5. Select and apply a theological construct.
  6. State a conclusion.
  7. Offer your decision that correlates with your conclusion. That is, describe what you would do in a sentence or two. All briefs must include a decision.

EXERCISE 2

From your analysis of "No Ordinary Sunday" in Exercise 1, write a one-page case brief.

As a student, the case method will enhance your ability to manage the various routine and unexpected demands of serving churches. However, learning to write cases from your own lived experiences will increase your capacity to reflect theologically about ministerial practice. By employing a model of ministerial reflection (see chapter 3), the critical incident you chose to write about will become a learning tool that will facilitate your growth. And when you share your own case with a peer reflection group, with a mentor, or in a classroom setting, you open your life to a transformative moment.

Writing a Case

Case studies allow you to examine the lived experiences of others. People tell narratives to make sense of life and experience. Once you have read and analyzed several cases, you begin to feel the impact that this method has for your future teaching and learning. To grow in your use of the case method, you will need to write your own case. When you are reflecting upon the experiences of others through the cases they have written, your ability to incorporate many pastoral practices and integrate ministerial wisdom grows. Now, by writing about your own lived experiences, your professional identity will also continue to develop.

A case is a written description of an authentic event that is fraught with ambiguity. The identities of people, places, and institutions are changed to protect their privacy. The case does not provide all conceivable information, because no one could know everything that happened or what everyone thought. Enough data is provided so that your reader can enter vicariously into the situation. A case is seen through the eyes of one person, the protagonist, who must make a crucial decision about a real-world situation. The case is left open-ended; that is, the reader is not told what decision was made. The reader is expected to study the case and enter into the experience and dilemma of the central character. The basic question becomes, what would I do? The focus in the case method is about owning one's decisions and developing an intelligible rationale for one's stance.

Literary theory is a helpful conversation partner when you first begin to write a case. Most people tell their stories in smaller segments often called episodes. Sometimes the episodes are sequenced according to themes or, more common, time (chronology). When the story is told, episodes are excluded or included depending upon the purpose and place of the telling. Selection—what episode choices are made for inclusion and exclusion—plays a major role in shaping the content of the narratives. A common narrative sequence as old as Aristotle's Poetics involves conflict, complication, climax, and resolution (denouement). The conflict describes the dilemma, an issue or incident that has no apparent way forward. The great white shark eats the unsuspecting swimmer. Next, the plot thickens through complicating circumstances. The white shark is smarter and stronger than any previously encountered. The usual methods for capturing the beast have resulted in more loss of human life and the local tourist economy is devastated. Eventually, the story line reaches the crucial point of decision and action. From here, there is no going back. Either the great shark hunter succeeds or all is doomed. And then comes the finale. The shark is destroyed, and all people along the coast are saved.

The case study interrupts the plot sequence by leaving the resolution open. The climax of the story is suspended for reflection purposes. Furthermore, stories express the multiplicity of meaning and the interconnectedness of phenomena that resist reducing life to simple formulas, facts, and singular interpretations. Stories accommodate the ambiguity and inconsistency found in everyday experience. By leaving open the rest of the story, you provide your peers the opportunity to grapple with a wide range of possible and reasonable pastoral interventions. If a reflection group analyzing the case takes a different route to resolution than you did, then the possibilities to assess your decisions and actions multiply.

I use the following handout when I am instructing students about writing their first case or when I need to be reminded of the basics.

BASIC GUIDELINES FOR CASE WRITING

- A good case describes a difficult problem, a dilemma for which no single obvious solution exists. If the solution is obvious, or if the courses of possible action would not produce a difference of opinion, then you do not have the material for a good case. Choose an event or situation that poses a question and requires a decision fraught with sufficient difficulty and ambiguity so that people of intelligence and sensitivity will disagree about what ought to be done. The case can be based on historical events or on personal experiences. Cases that are multifaceted yet reasonably short are most effective.

- A case must describe an actual, not a hypothetical, situation. Nothing will draw participants into the discussion of a case more quickly and intensely than assurance that it really happened or is happening. It may be necessary to disguise a case by changing names or places, but avoid exaggerations, embellishments, or alterations that could prompt readers to doubt the accuracy or truthfulness of the case itself. Select a case in which the participants will be willing to provide you with the information you need to describe the background, the individuals involved, the situation of the dilemma itself, and the possible courses of action. If you write about a personal experience, you will be the source of information.

- A case should be about a question or problem with which many people can identify and in which they have genuine interest. Ask yourself, will the discussion of the case benefit those I will ask to study and discuss it? Early in the process of writing a case, determine your audience, goals, and themes.

- A case is written from one person's perspective. Avoid seeing it through the eyes of everyone involved. Do not attribute feelings or motives to anyone in the case unless the person involved verbalizes them. To write a case from one person's perspective may appear too narrow and exclusive, yet it is how we perceive reality, and we must make decisions based on the limited facts and data available to us.

- A case is a distinct literary form. It is a genre with rules and conventions. It has a certain structure. It is not just a photographic slice of life. A case represents episodes selected from a particular situation by the case writer and is outlined as follows:

1. *Focus*: The first paragraph sets up the dilemma. The case begins with the suspended climax of the plot. The cliffhanger is posed from the outset.
2. *Background*: The next few paragraphs give the setting and history of the case so that the dilemma is understood. All participants would agree about this material. Include sufficient information to give the reader an adequate feeling for the case situation without including unnecessary details. Dialogue, letters, or appendices may be helpful tools in this section of the case. The literary device of flashback is commonly used. In literature, internal *analepsis* is a flashback to an earlier point in the narrative; external analepsis is a flashback to a time before the narrative started.
3. *Development* (the plot thickens): The next several paragraphs develop the plot. Decide whose eyes the case will be seen through. Use limited third person as opposed to omniscient (the all-seeing) perspective. Select material with the case dilemma in mind by interweaving time structure, plot, character development, and action. Do not portray any characters so negatively that others cannot relate to their experience.
4. *Coda*: The last paragraph (or paragraphs) rephrases or highlights the issue or decision. The coda is an *inclusio* with the first paragraph of the case. Like bookends, the first and last paragraphs frame the case by highlighting the dilemma. Ask yourself whether the cutoff point is a good one. Try to avoid ending with a question. Allow the power of suspending the story at a climactic point, a type of cliffhanger, to function to create tension in the reader. Done well, the reader will seek resolution.

- Pay attention to points of style:
1. Provide a clear chronology.
2. Check transition points for clarity.
3. Try to be an objective reporter of known facts.
4. Ascribe opinions to those who make them.
5. Quote when possible.

6. Avoid editorializing.
7. Keep adverbs and adjectives to a minimum.
8. Report body language and physical setting to build reader interest and involvement.
9. Present the case in the past tense.
10. Avoid cute names for characters and places when disguising identity so that the tone of the case will evoke serious attention.

EXERCISE 3

Write a case study that emerges from your ministry experience. Start with a short scenario before tackling more complex story lines.

Presenting a Case

Earlier, I described writing a case brief as a formal way to synthesize your analysis of a case. Learning to present a case to a small group or class also develops your understanding of the case and augments your integration of the wisdom garnered from the case into your practice. Because case teaching is such a powerful method for communal discernment, many pastors have found it an effective tool in their own ministries. Church consultants in various disciplines have successfully used cases to mediate the difficult terrain in their respective fields. Learning to present a case in a formal setting will give you a pedagogical tool that you can effectively utilize throughout your tenure as a minister.

Before you present your first case, inform your supervisor-mentor of your teaching plan one day prior to the scheduled class time. There is no substitute for careful planning, and the feedback from an experienced case teacher is priceless. It is customary for an effective teaching plan to cover approximately two hours in order to allow enough time for the group to analyze and reflect upon the case. I use the following handout to describe a typical teaching plan.

A TEACHING PLAN

(Total class time: 120 minutes)

- *Learning Objectives*: Learning objectives are the tentative outcomes you expect to achieve during the case presentation. Spell out two to four learning objectives that utilize strong verbs. Possible verbs include: *affirm, encourage, demonstrate, synthesize, analyze, appraise, apply, compare and contrast, differentiate, discriminate, prepare, formulate, design, construct, assess, evaluate,* and *value*. Imagine the possible alternatives. From a list of issues within a single case, various pedagogical aims can be achieved. From a single case, applications are possible from the fields of conflict resolution, leadership, pastoral care, social justice, and missions. A New Testament professor may use the context of a case to engage a class on hermeneutics. A homiletics professor may compare and contrast different scenarios in order to demonstrate the potential of a single text in various contexts. The list is endless and is determined by the particular learning outcomes the teacher has for the students. State these objectives clearly.
- *Distribute the Case*: Allow the group enough time to read the case. (10 minutes)
- *Brainstorming Activity 1—Characters*: Using a white board or large sticky notes, list all the characters involved in the case. Note two to three key identifying characteristics. (10 minutes)
- *Brainstorming Activity 2—Issues*: On a different board or sticky notes, list the issues that emerge from the case. When you suggest an issue, note from what part of the case you deem that it emerges. Ask, "For which of our characters is this issue critical?" (15 minutes)
- *Possible Active Learning Strategies*
    1. Mini-Lecture. A mini-lecture may be delivered before, during, or after the case presentation when appropriate. The lecturer should not preempt the discussion or cut it off by giving the "right answer." Alternative: A guest speaker, resource person, or podcast could be utilized to give a mini-lecture or presentation. (10 minutes)

2. Small Groups. Small-group discussions may provide opportunities for full participation by all those present. The group assignment must be clear, and the teaching plan must allow sufficient time for them to discuss and then to return to the larger gathering. (Pair and Share is another form of small-group discussion that gets everyone involved by simply asking everyone to team up with his or her neighbor.) For example: Divide the class into groups, each representing either one of the characters or a particular issue. Provide the groups with markers and sticky notes so that they can record their discussion. Ask them to do the following (30 minutes):
   a. Select an issue that emerged in the earlier discussion, one you deem vital for your character to consider.
   b. Discuss what is most at stake for your character.
   c. Discuss some of the alternative decisions or actions available to your character.
   d. Identify possible resources available to your character.
3. Role Play. Role play is often a good follow-up activity to a small-group discussion. Ask the group to discuss possible talking points for the group's assigned character. Pick one person in the group to come in front of the class and play the character. Provide the selected students with large name tags. Reenact or create a scenario for the characters. After the role play, thank the actors. Debrief with the whole class by asking one to two key questions. (20 minutes)
4. Voting or Polling. Asking participants to vote on a key issue before the discussion begins can energize a conversation about the rationale for and implications of various positions. Continuing with "the minority report" (using the opinion of the minority rather than the majority) is often useful. When voting or polling is used, the participants may be divided into pro and con groups. The students' votes place them into two groups that would prepare a point-counterpoint discussion about one of the selected issues.

5. Fishbowl. Fishbowl is a device that allows the facilitator to select a small group of participants (or allow them to volunteer) to discuss pertinent issues, ideas, and solutions in front of the class. The rest of the group listens to the conversation. One modification of this approach is to allow small groups to choose a spokesperson to present the group's discussion. Another is to leave one chair in the discussion circle empty so that listening participants can move in and out of the discussion. In addition, chairs could be labeled to represent certain characters.
6. Jigsaw. Jigsaw is a means of giving individuals with different information or perspectives an opportunity to share with others. For example, if participants are divided into small groups, and each group is given a different topic, issue, or character to discuss, they spend a designated period completing their assignment. They are then regrouped so that a representative from each small group is included in the new small groups.

- *Wrap-up*: Develop a concluding activity that brings closure to the presentation. For example, you might distribute a questionnaire: (1) What have we learned from this case? (2) Choose one character. How would you handle the situation? (3) What wisdom do we as interns garner from the case? The purpose of the questionnaire (or a final writing assignment) allows the student to concisely describe how they understand the case and what concrete lessons they will apply to their own practice in the future.
- *Thank everyone for participating.*

EXERCISE 4

From the bibliography, select and teach a case in a peer reflection group. Ask your supervisor-mentor to serve as a nonparticipant observer who will give you critical feedback on your performance.

Many case facilitators advise not teaching your own case. The opportunity for greater learning occurs when you observe someone else teach your case.

Continual attention to faculty development is a key component to your growth as an academic professional. Writing and presenting case studies enhances your portfolio. More important, significant impact upon student maturation is facilitated through effective implementation of the case method. Teaching a student to exercise pastoral ministry within the life of the church is like teaching an artist to paint. The classroom provides the student with a focused opportunity not only to paint but also to show others how to paint. As the teacher engages students in the classroom, she will mold their giftedness by mixing in some craft along the way. She will guide, encourage, and allow students to continue the process of becoming who they are called by God to be and to reflect the incarnate Word within the larger community. The teacher's pastoral leadership will encourage students to become distinct voices within community, witnessing to their experience of the gospel and their maturation in Christ.

5

The Power of Reflecting with Peers

DONNA R. DUENSING

Joshua comes into the office expressing his doubts. He felt confident that God was calling him to ministry, but he just didn't feel his gifts measured up to those of others in his class. He could list the accomplishments of other students, but he saw only his own shortcomings. It was clear that he didn't see in himself what I and others saw in him.

This is an all too common occurrence. We can trace this human predicament all the way back to Moses. Remember that conversation between Moses and God: "But God, I've never been very good at this public speaking bit, and now you want me to speak for you?" God responds by telling Moses that he will tell him what to say (Exod. 4:10–12).

Have you been in Joshua's or Moses' shoes? When that strong internal critic rents too much space in your brain, trusting your giftedness is difficult. This is when you need to hear God speaking to you through the community. Peer groups are an excellent venue in which to cultivate an atmosphere where you can be affirmed and encouraged to become everything God has created you to be. Your tendencies to see only the places where you don't measure up to your own expectations will be kept in check by your peers, who will be able to hold up a mirror and reflect back to you the unique gifts God has given you. They can nurture your true self, and with that authenticity integrated into your practice of ministry, your vocational formation will flourish.

It is easy to fall prey to comparisons. Consider the story of Moses, the leader. It is easy to imagine someone wishing to emulate Moses. But Moses worried about not being an eloquent speaker and questioned God's wisdom in calling him. God dismissed his excuses and instead promised that he would not be alone. God would provide Aaron, his brother, to help him. Most important, God pledges to be with him. This is also true for you. You need not try to be like one of your classmates or an ideal in your imagination or even a Moses. God has called you as you are and will further develop your gifts through seminary and beyond. Cultivating the practice of reflecting with peers is a powerful antidote to attempts to be anyone other than who you are by nature and by grace.

You are created to live in community. God gives you partners in ministry. In the practice of ministry, you are connected to God's life source through peer groups. Some of these groups develop naturally and organically. Thanks be to God when that happens! Other times you will need to create peer groups to support you in your vocational formation process.

The power of peer reflection is a resource for student and supervisor-mentor alike. This is a lifelong power source for ministry. Good practices during the seminary years will develop into habits that will serve you throughout your professional life. Through the various reflection groups of which you are a part, you will discover what is needed in a group to make it a safe place to share your vulnerabilities and your strengths. You will find the methods that best enable you to uncover your gifts and develop your ministry skills.

In this chapter, I invite you not only to look at the various opportunities for peer reflection within the educational structure and to be intentional in utilizing these groups but also to create your own peer groups.

For Students: Making the Most of Required Peer-Reflection Groups

It is important to be intentional about reflecting with peers. The curriculum in most theological schools offers a variety of formal reflection groups. Approaching these requirements as merely hoops to jump through or items to check off the list is dangerous. I encourage you to use each of these opportunities to learn more about group process and to become a competent group member. This will enable you to gain even more than the stated outcomes of these classes. Each of these groups will provide its own guidelines or covenants for group formation. Finding effective formats for group interactions is valuable. Ask yourself what dynamics are needed to make this an environment for your personal and vocational growth. Make mental notes about what is important to you in order to build trust and acceptance, and foster good communication.

Clinical Pastoral Education (CPE) is a great opportunity to explore a variety of types of interactions. The Association for Clinical Pastoral Education standards for Interpersonal Relations Groups have been developed over the years and will provide a model for how a diverse group can affirm and further the development of each individual in the group through an agreed-upon process and focus. This educational model will give you tools for structuring reflection, such as bringing prepared critical incidents reports and verbatims to the group and soliciting specific feedback for your growth areas.

When membership in the group is assigned rather then self-selected, interactions can be challenging, especially if some members are coming from a different theological or political perspective than you. This is the time to check in with yourself and examine your primary reaction mode. Do you withdraw or shut down? Do you spend all your energy thinking about your rebuttal rather than deeply listening to the other point of view? Do you attempt to find allies who are ready to join you in battle?

You will receive the greatest benefit if you work to find ways to engage in healthy dialogue with individuals who have different opinions. A diverse group will give you an effective lab in which to gain understanding of another person's position as well as your own. Later when you encounter similar polarizing positions in your congregation or ministry sites, you will have a new lens for understanding.

In these formal prearranged groups, you will encounter a wide range of interpersonal skills among group members. It can be frustrating if any of the group members lack commitment to the group's covenant. If this happens, again, do your own personal check-in. What is your response? What group leadership skills might you implement to reengage the members? In what ways can you build healthy coalitions within the group to improve the effectiveness of the discussions?

GROUND RULES AND RESOURCES

There are many approaches to peer-group covenants. Some basic commitments are necessary in these agreements. These include, but are not limited to, the following:

- Be prompt and faithful in attendance.
- Participate fully, in both speaking *and* listening.
- Respect the other members of the group.
- Confidentiality: what happens in the room, stays in the room.
- Be responsible and own your own feelings and opinions (that is, use "I" statements).

> **SAMPLE PEER-GROUP COVENANT FROM WESTERN THEOLOGICAL SEMINARY**
>
> I declare my intention to be a faithful participant in my peer group.
>
> As a faithful participant, I will attend every group meeting. If an emergency should prevent my attending, I will notify another group member or the facilitator.

I will recognize that the central purpose of our meeting is to develop a spirit of collegiality and mutual growth that will undergird and enhance our seminary experience.

I will hold confidential all that occurs in our group meetings, even from those outside the group whom I feel I can trust.

I will communicate honestly about my experiences in my Teaching Church, in the classroom, and in my personal life, even those that seem like failure, recognizing that these are the experiences from which I can most readily enlarge my understanding of my role in ministry.

I will demonstrate respect for my colleagues by letting them see me as I am, not solely as I would like to be seen. I will demonstrate trust by allowing my colleagues their right to their privacy, when they so choose.

I will seek opportunities to affirm and support my colleagues.

I will recognize the presence of God with us in all of our doing—in our struggles and our perplexities, in our joy and in our laughter, in our personal and in our professional growth—not confining my sense of God's presence to times of worship but recognizing that the Spirit of God is continually among us where two or three meet to search for ways to encourage and deepen growth and ministry in our part of God's world.[1]

_____Peer Group Member

_____Date

The following "Seven Principles of Fierce Conversations" by Susan Scott, a leadership developer, from her book *Fierce Conversations* provide valuable insights for all conversations and could be especially useful in your peer groups.[2]

1. *Master the courage to interrogate reality.* No plan survives its collision with reality, and reality has a habit of shifting, at work and at home. Markets and economies change, requiring shifts in strategy. People change and forget to tell each other—colleagues, customers, spouses, friends. We are all changing all the time. Not only do we neglect to share this with others, we are skilled at masking it even to ourselves.

2. *Come out from behind yourself into the conversation and make it real.* While many fear "real," it is the unreal conversation that should scare us to death. Unreal conversations are expensive, for the individual and the organization. No one has to change, but everyone has to have the conversation. When the conversation is real, the change occurs before the conversation is over. You will accomplish your goals in large part by making every conversation you have as real as possible.

3. *Be here, prepared to be nowhere else.* Our work, our relationships, and our lives succeed or fail one conversation at a time. While no single conversation is guaranteed to transform a company, a relationship, or a life, any single conversation can. Speak and listen as if this is the most important conversation you will ever have with this person. It could be. Participate as if it matters. It does.

4. *Tackle your toughest challenge today.* Burnout doesn't occur because we are solving problems; it occurs because we have been trying to solve the same problem over and over. The problem named is the problem solved. Identify and then confront the real obstacles in your path. Stay current with the people important to your success and happiness. Travel light, agenda-free.

5. *Obey your instincts.* Don't just trust your instincts—obey them. Your radar screen works perfectly. It is the operator who is in question. An intelligence agent is sending you messages every day, all day. Tune in. Pay attention. Share these thoughts with others. What we label as illusion is the scent of something real coming close.

6. *Take responsibility for your emotional wake.* For a leader, there is no trivial comment. Something you don't remember saying may have had a devastating impact on someone who looked to you for guidance and approval. The conversation is not about the relationship; the conversation is the relationship. Learning to deliver the message without the load allows you to speak with clarity, conviction, and compassion.

7. *Let the silence do the heavy lifting.* When there is simply a whole lot of talking going on, conversations can be so empty of meaning they crackle. Memorable conversations include breathing space. Slow down the conversation, so that insight can occur in the space between words and you can discover what the conversation really wants and needs to be about.

For Students: Thriving Informal Peer Groups

Perhaps the most powerful, life-giving peer groups will be those of your own creation. In this age of ever-expanding social networking, you have many opportunities for forming groups. However, it is important to offer a word of caution about how these groups are formed and for what purpose. Your Facebook wall is not the place to discuss formation, vocational, or ministry issues. A healthy group of peers who are available to you for confidential discussions will help you maintain appropriate boundaries in more public venues.

In chapter 7, "Self-Care and Community," in this book, contributor Jaco Hamman quotes his favorite African proverb about relationships. It compares friends to moss: "The metaphor suggests someone is protected from the wounds of life or heals faster if friends and a community are part of that person's life." Informal peer groups can be "life-giving moss." Covenanting with friends to be in a peer-group relationship is invaluable.

These relationships can grow out of other groups of which you have been a member. I know of students who began a covenant peer group in seminary and then agreed to continue to meet once a year in retreat to reflect on vocational and ministry issues. The trust and intimacy that developed through the years became a powerful, life-giving support. In another situation, members of a summer CPE group agreed to meet several times in the years following their unit of CPE. They realized that the knowledge they had of each other's vocational journey and the bond of trust that had developed would be invaluable as they continued their vocational journeys. A colleague of mine was a member of this group. She told me that even though more than a decade has passed, she still calls on a member of this group to coach her on ministry issues.

In seminary, particular affinity groups can be helpful. Some are short term and task oriented, like a study or project group. Field education students serving in similar contexts, such as urban ministries, or chaplaincies, find it helpful to gather for reflection on their practice of ministry. At our school, interns who are scattered across the country during their yearlong internship frequently set up a list serve so that they can remain connected. To receive the greatest benefits, covenant with your peers to point out the areas where you need to stretch. Being challenged and at the same time affirmed can be valuable.

I trust one of my dearest friends, whom I have known since seminary days, to be open and honest with me when she notices behaviors that can signal unconscious struggles. She will say something like, "I noticed that you are worried about money. Are you anxious about something?" She knows me well enough to know that my free-floating anxiety fixates on finances when money may have nothing to do with it. Having a friend that will give you honest feedback is a precious resource.

Who are your precious resources? Just as God promised Moses that he would not be left alone, you will not be left alone. Treasure your peers, your friends who know you, affirm you, stretch you, and love you. Formalize your connections. They are powerful connections. They can save your life.

For Supervisors and Mentors

Actions often do speak louder than words. As a supervisor or mentor, your modeling of the importance of peer groups will speak volumes. This will not mean that the field education student will be a member of your peer groups. However, if you share how these groups have served you, the student will benefit from your witness.

If you discover that you don't have many healthy peer groups to talk about, let it be a warning sign to you. Many forces can lead to your becoming isolated. Clergy are warned about becoming friends with congregants. Also, the demands of ministry easily carve into a minister's personal life, which leaves little time and energy for nurturing relationships with colleagues and friends. As a result, many pastors describe themselves as being lonely. Some leaders become lone rangers in ministry. Neither of these positions is healthy for effective leadership.

If these feelings of isolation are familiar to you, now is the time to reconnect to your friends and peers. Reconnect to those valued colleagues who remind you of your giftedness, those trusted friends who know and love you enough to tell you when your stresses and anxieties are showing.

There may be peer groups—ministerial groups, text studies, or interfaith groups—that you and your ministry student can attend together. Participating together provides the opportunity to reflect on group dynamics. Ask each other what made a particular interaction helpful and healthy. Together you can strategize on ways the two of you might strengthen a group.

As a supervisor, taking advantage of meetings when other mentors and supervisors of ministry are present, or forming a peer group of area supervisors, will develop your supervisory gifts. These meetings will provide the opportunity to share resources and encourage and affirm one another. Bringing difficult or challenging issues to the group for their reflections and feedback provides an opportunity to tap into shared wisdom.

Some theological institutions provide opportunity for leaders of supervised ministry settings to gather with faculty to discuss current issues in ministry. These groups provide new insights and connections with what professors are addressing in their courses and allow faculty to receive helpful feedback. These interactions are rich opportunities for the supervisors and faculty to find new resources for their professional growth. It strengthens the connections between the academic and practical worlds.

God with You

God knows you better than you know yourself. Through the power of reflecting with peers, you can see and hear the gifts God has given you. You have blind sides where your talents remain hidden from you, and sometimes you discount your natural gifts and skill. When that happens, peer reflection can be the voice of God calling you fully into your true vocational identity. These communities rest on holy ground. The interactions are sacred. Within these groups, your vocational formation becomes the ongoing creative work of God. To be an active, engaged member of such groups is an opportunity to be a cocreator. That is a *wonder*-full and *power*-full experience!

6
The Forming Work of Congregations

LEE CARROLL

When Betsy Thayer began her Master of Divinity degree program, she was no recent college graduate. She had been discerning her call to ordained ministry for more than ten years, and during that time she served as a deacon and in countless other roles with her congregation. She felt that she already knew what was involved in leading a congregation. So she was hoping that her seminary would waive the field education requirement for her degree. "After all," she said, "I've been there and done that!"

Her classmate Jim Rucker was equally resistant to the field education requirement. While he was younger than Betsy—just one year out of college—and knew little about being a pastor, he was clear that he was being called to be a hospital chaplain. What could he possibly learn from doing an internship in a congregation that might prepare him for his future as a chaplain?

Jordan Freeman was still discerning his vocation, and while he was open to doing an internship with a congregation, he was very anxious about doing so. He had attended church only occasionally as a teenager and had almost no idea about how congregations functioned. He generally saw himself as a seeker who could find his way more readily through academic work—but certainly not in a pastoral internship where he might make a fool of himself.

While Betsy, Jim, and Jordan are fictional characters, their stories are very common. Students enter seminaries every year with a wide range of needs and views. Some are experienced in congregational life and assume they have seen it all. Some are focused on pursuing ministerial vocations outside of congregational settings. Others have had no pastoral experience or lack vocational clarity. But they represent many theological students who question the value of a congregation-based internship as part of their theological education.

This chapter seeks to make a case for the congregation as an indispensable partner with the theological school in forming people for ministry—not only for leading congregations but also for other forms of service for God's mission. Indeed, congregations—with all their struggles and issues, in all their many and varied forms—continue to be the most basic way that people of faith gather, and as such, they provide an amazingly rich context for discerning ways that God is at work in the world. Theologian Robert Schreiter writes, "What makes congregations the special places they are is that they are focused on God, in whom they live, move, and have their being. Their members congregate to remember how God has acted in the history of the world and in their own lives. They congregate to discern what is happening to them and to the world today, and to listen for where God is leading them. Theology is an expression of the relation between God and such congregations of faithful, seeking people."[1]

Schreiter's insight regarding the nature of the congregational context is critical. While ministry in the larger world context is always a faithful response to the gospel, congregations make a unique contribution to ministerial formation because of their commitment to the vocation of theological discernment.

The Congregation as a Context for Theological Education

In one way or another, all congregational practices are based upon theological convictions. Some of these beliefs are quite explicit or visible; others remain more implicit or unspoken. Regardless, one of your key responsibilities as a supervisor-mentor or an intern is to read and respond to the various theological values being expressed through the life and mission of your congregation. This is a core responsibility of any pastoral leader.

Implicit theologies tend to be more difficult to recognize, but they often form the theological underbelly of a congregation.[2] Many of them are private beliefs held by members that are based largely upon unexamined childhood convictions handed down from parents, teachers, and others. Although such beliefs may not be found in the congregation's public documents, they often surface in strong ways during times of conflict, dividing members and paralyzing the missional vision of the congregation. By contrast, *explicit theologies* are more readily expressed through the more public declarations of the congregation such as mission statements, liturgies, oft-sung hymns, creeds, denominational confessional statements, and other published documents.

One of the realities you will discover is that implicit and explicit theologies sometimes compete with one another within a congregation. As with our personal lives, congregations must guard against inconsistencies between private convictions and public actions, consciously pursuing integrity within the community of faith. Otherwise, members will find themselves confused about who they are and what theological values they are transmitting through their life and mission together. When a congregation consistently preaches the importance of serving the poor but never gets around to working with or for the poor, or when a congregation advertises that "everyone is welcome" but members are inhospitable to visitors, their theologies are conflicted.

So, what is the best starting place for doing theology in your congregation? A very common approach is to begin with a theological doctrine and to apply it to the realities or practices of the congregation—a process that Christian educator Thomas Groome calls the "theory-to-practice paradigm." Regrettably, when some clergy apply this theological model in their congregations, they do so in a rather strong-handed way, suggesting that theology is a domain reserved for pastors or academics—but not the laity. In this approach, as Groom suggests, "theology is done either *for the people* or *to the people*," but not *by the people*.[3]

Another starting point reverses the theory-to-practice model. Commonly called "practical theology," this approach begins by examining the concrete situation of a particular congregation, then critiques this situation in light of the biblical story, and ultimately seeks a new vision or course of action. In time, these newly discerned visions or actions must be subjected to ongoing theological scrutiny, as the community continues to discern the will of God. In this approach to doing theology with the people, there is a clear and compelling relationship between congregational practices and theological tradition. To borrow from an image in storytelling, practical theology seeks to bring congregational narratives into conformity with biblical narratives.

The following example illustrates the process of practical theology: leaders in one congregation became increasingly frustrated with their quarterly observance of Eucharist. Some wondered why it seemed so somber and funeral-like; others noted that it seemed like an add-on to worship. So, over an extended time they delved into relevant biblical texts and confessional statements. After considerable prayer and study, the congregation concluded that while their current sacramental emphasis on remembering Jesus's Last Supper and Good Friday was appropriate, other equally appropriate understandings of Eucharist were also valued within their tradition—new theological understandings that focused more on Easter and the great heavenly banquet. Subsequently, the congregation diversified its way of celebrating the sacrament, sometimes using the traditional approach, sometimes using a liturgy that reflected their new theological insights.

One significant advantage to the approach of practical theology is that it encourages *communal* discernment and leadership. In keeping with the priesthood of all believers, practical theology brings clergy and laity together for discerning the activity of God in the world today. When people are invited to participate in such ongoing theological reflections, the possibility that they will commit themselves to growing through shared theological disciplines and to the congregation's role in God's mission is much greater.

Understanding Your Congregation

As a supervisor-mentor or pastoral intern, how can you grow in your capacity for understanding the ministry context in which you are serving? How can you gain critical insights about the theology being lived out by those with whom you are serving? These are competencies that are important for ministry in any setting, but they are essential for those who serve with congregations.

Practical theologians working in the field of congregational studies have developed valuable insights and resources that can help us address this need. In *Studying Congregations*,[4] Nancy Ammerman, sociology of religion scholar, and colleagues have described four very helpful lenses or approaches to understanding the concrete situation of a congregation: cultural, ecological, process, and resources. While using any one of these lenses might reveal important insights, one single lens is seldom as valuable as all four used together.

The following is a collection of field-tested, practical exercises that supervisor-mentors and interns can use for theological discernment with members of their congregation. Each suggested process is grouped under one of the four frames identified above by Ammerman and her colleagues.

Culture Lens: Congregational Identity

One of the four approaches to understanding the situation of your congregation focuses on its identity or internal culture—its history, rituals, beliefs, values, artifacts, stories, myths, ways of dealing with visitors, and other factors that distinguish your congregation from others. Here are three possible exercises to use in understanding the *culture* of your congregation: congregational timeline, artifacts and places, and typologies.

CONGREGATIONAL TIMELINE

This exercise involves members in developing an overview of the congregation's history. Using a large chalkboard or several pieces of newsprint, draw a long, horizontal line across the middle of the surface. At the far left of the line, note the founding year of the church; and at the far right, note the current year. Then, beginning with the past and working forward by decades, invite the group to tell the story of the congregation as they have heard or remembered it. Record major events, "glory days," crises, and other turning points below the line. If the history is long, you can abbreviate the process by reviewing only the most recent thirty to forty years. Above the line, note community or world events that had an effect on the congregation's story. After the story is recorded, identify long-term values from the story that continue to shape the identity of the congregation.

ARTIFACTS AND PLACES

Clues about congregational identity are also found in the artifacts or places that members hold dear or sacred. Someone has suggested that if you want to learn whether something is sacred to members, just move it! One congregation voted to relocate the organ from the front of the sanctuary to the rear gallery, only to have one woman resign her church membership in protest, complaining, "I just can't worship God in a place like this!" Interns and supervisors can explore congregational culture by working with a group of church members to identify special places or artifacts that hold deeply emotional meaning for members. Discuss what these artifacts and places symbolize and how they have come to have sacred meaning.

TYPOLOGIES

Congregations can be classified in numerous ways. Some congregational categories are sociological in nature—for example, denominations, social locations, or size. But other typologies like the one developed by theologian H. Richard Niebuhr in *Christ and Culture* are more theological. He identified five ways that congregations view their cultural context: (1) Christ against Culture, (2) Christ of Culture, (3) Christ above Culture, (4) Christ and Culture in Paradox, and (5) Christ Transforming Culture.[5]

Another theological typology was developed by David Roozen, William McKinney, and Jackson Carroll,[6] who constructed a simple matrix that maps four different mission orientations of congregations. On one axis of their grid, congregations are categorized either as "This-Worldly" or "Other-Worldly" in their theology; and on the other axis, they are described either as "Membership-Centered" or "Publicly Proactive" in their approach to ministry. Accordingly, four different mission orientations—civic, sanctuary, activist, and evangelistic—are defined as follows:

Civic orientation (this-worldly theology combined with membership-centered ministry)—affirms existing social structures; avoids confrontations in the public arena. Members are encouraged to make own decisions on social issues.

Sanctuary orientation (other-worldly theology combined with membership-centered ministry)—fosters patriotism and adherence to civil law; sees the congregation as refuge from the world. Members resist involvement in social change.

Activist orientation (this-worldly theology combined with publicly proactive ministry)—stresses justice; takes a critical posture toward existing social structures. Members, individually and collectively, engage in social action.

Evangelistic orientation (other-worldly theology combined with publicly proactive ministry)—stresses personal witnessing and sharing their faith with others. Members seek to convert others to the "one true faith."

With a group of congregants, review these four mission orientations or Niebuhr's categories from *Christ and Culture*, and ask them to identify the ones that best describe your congregation's views. Inviting individual members to locate themselves within one or more of these typologies often reveals critical patterns about how the congregation understands its mission.

Ecological Lens: Congregational Context

A second approach to studying your congregation's situation is to examine its social context—its neighborhood, its larger region, its denomination, and its socioeconomic or political environment.

The impact of social context upon any congregation is powerful. To illustrate, one neighborhood congregation found itself struggling to survive anticipated neighborhood changes. The city school board had recently announced plans to close the local elementary school, and soon afterward the state department of transportation proposed building a new freeway that would cut through the middle of this once-vibrant community. The results were predictable. Property values plummeted overnight. Many church members moved away, leaving the remnant to wonder if the congregation would even survive. The crisis deepened further when their long-term pastor retired. But what happened next was truly amazing. After an extended search, a new pastor was called and began her work with the troubled congregation. Ironically, one month later, both the school board *and* transportation officials announced that they were dropping their controversial plans. Immediately the neighborhood became a real-estate hot spot and people swarmed back into the community. The congregation swelled with new members, and within a year, they were not only stable but also growing. Understandably, the pastor was seen as a Moses figure who had guided them out of their wilderness. While the new pastor was an excellent leader, she would be the first to point out that the most important factor in their survival was the resurgence of their neighborhood. Indeed, the external environment had done its magic on the congregation.

Here are three possible exercises to use in exploring the influences of social context (ecological lens) upon the life of your congregation: the neighborhood drive or walk, asset mapping, and analysis of demographic data.

THE NEIGHBORHOOD DRIVE OR WALK

Many members may live outside the neighborhood of their congregation and thus know it only as a visitor. One excellent way to familiarize them with the neighborhood is to take small groups of members on a neighborhood walk or drive. Arrange for the tour to include discussions with community residents and leaders. After the tour, reflect together on what you have seen and heard and identify an agenda for further study of the community.

ASSET MAPPING

What are the assets of the neighborhood where your congregation serves? John Kretzmann and John McKnight, both research scholars with the Asset-Based Community Development Institute at Northwestern University, argue that while traditional approaches to community development focus on neighborhood problems, focusing on community assets is more productive. Instead of beginning with crime rates, poverty, and other issues, Kretzmann and McKnight encourage you to identify and map community resources that can be used for promoting the common good. Their text *Building Communities from the Inside Out* is a highly regarded resource to guide such a project.[7]

A modest variation on this approach is simply to develop a map of key assets within a three-mile circumference of the church building. Who lives there? Who works there? How do people living and working nearby view your congregation? How can your congregation become an even greater asset in the community?

ANALYSIS OF DEMOGRAPHIC DATA

A wealth of information is available online that can inform congregational leaders about the neighborhood. Some denominational judicatories subscribe to web-based demographic products and planning resources developed by organizations such as Percept[8] or Visions Decisions,[9] which provide demographic data on targeted geographical areas. The U.S. Census also provides invaluable public information, and it is free.[10] Such tools provide a snapshot of who lives in a census tract. Categories include race and ethnicity, gender, and age as well as income levels, employment percentages, housing types, and more. You might examine the demographic data for your neighborhood and name realities that have an impact your congregation's interactions with the community. What surprises are found in the data? What population trends or transitions should be considered in the congregation's planning for mission?

Process Lens: Congregational Dynamics

A third lens for studying your congregation involves examining the internal processes used within the congregation—decision making, conflict modes, leadership styles, and other social dynamics that shape the morale and climate of the congregation. As congregational studies experts Carl Dudley and Speed Leas have suggested, "Process is not what happens, but *how it happens*."[11] This way of viewing your congregation builds upon the insights of organizational development and family systems theory and applies these understandings to congregations.

An elder in one small congregation observed, "We may decide on a certain course of action in our monthly board meeting, but the *real* decisions are made afterward in the church parking lot!" This illustrates an important distinction between formal and informal processes used in congregations.[12] *Formal processes* are open, public considerations that are normally summarized in minutes or other records. Conversely, *informal processes* are actions that congregants actually follow outside the stated policies. Deep tensions can surface in congregations when formal and informal processes compete with one another for authority.

The following exercises are ways to explore your congregation through the process lens: planning and evaluating, dealing with conflict, and leadership styles.

PLANNING AND EVALUATING

How does your congregation go about planning and evaluating its work? Is it done formally by gathering information, assessing progress toward established goals, and developing strategic plans; or, are such formal processes viewed as a waste of time? It is important to discover basic attitudes about planning and evaluating and to identify who plays which role in these processes. A related exercise is to review the congregation's mission plan or vision statement, if any. How and when were these documents developed? Who was involved? Are they just archived documents with minimal visibility, or are they used routinely in planning and evaluating?

DEALING WITH CONFLICT

Individuals deal with conflict in numerous ways, but one classic analytical tool that can be easily adapted for use with your congregation is the *Thomas-Kilmann Conflict Mode Instrument*.[13] The theory behind this model is that a person's (or a congregation's) behavior in conflict situations is defined along two basic dimensions: *assertiveness*, that is, how aggressive you are in satisfying your concerns; and *cooperativeness*, how much you seek to satisfy the other person's concerns in a conflict. Based on how assertive and how cooperative you are, Thomas and Kilmann described five modes of dealing with conflict:

> *Competing*—assertive and uncooperative, this mode involves aggressively pursuing your own concerns at the expense of the other person.

Collaborating—assertive and cooperative, this mode involves your seeking to find a solution that satisfies both you and the other party.

Compromising—somewhat assertive and cooperative, this mode involves pursuing a mutually acceptable solution.

Avoiding—the opposite of collaborating, this mode is unassertive and uncooperative, and normally involves your disengaging from the conflict. It can be a way to postpone debate until a better time or place, or it can be a total withdrawal from a conflicted situation.

Accommodating—the opposite of competing, this mode is unassertive and cooperative and involves your sacrificing your own interests to satisfy the interests of other people or groups.

As with individuals, most congregations have a preferred style of dealing with conflicts. You can examine this by inviting congregants to recall conflicts in recent years and to identify the mode used with each. Are there trends? Did conflicts surface from role confusions, from controversial issues with no simple solution, from personality clashes, or from incompatible values or goals?[14] What can you learn about your congregation by describing the way it deals with conflict?

LEADERSHIP STYLES

Yet another aspect of congregational processes has to do with leadership styles. While no one style is appropriate for all situations, congregations do demonstrate preferred styles of leadership. Daniel Goleman, Richard Boyatzis, and Annie McKee,[15] researchers in the field of emotional intelligence, have described six basic leadership styles:

Visionary: Leaders move people toward shared dreams. This is most helpful when change in the congregation requires a new vision or clearer direction.

Coaching: Leaders connect individual members to the goals of the congregation. This often involves delegating responsibilities in order to build ownership.

Affiliative: Leaders create harmony in the congregation by connecting people to each other.

Democratic: Often used to build consensus, leaders place a high value on people's input and get commitment to congregational goals through participation. This works well when leaders are not clear on a course of action and need input from members.

Pacesetting: Leaders expect excellence and exemplify it. They push members to meet challenges and exciting goals.

Commanding: This is an authoritarian style. Leaders push others to move forward "because I say so!" This is logically used when in deep crisis situations or when no one has stepped forward with authority over a long period of time.

When you examine leadership styles at work in your congregation, the tendency is to focus on approaches used by the pastor, but lay leaders *also* exercise leadership. As an exercise in exploring this, review these six leadership models and ask whether your congregation generally has a clear preference for one or another of these styles. If your congregation needed a new pastor today, what kind of leader would they most likely seek? Why? Who are the most influential lay leaders in the congregation? What styles of leadership do they tend to use?

Resources Lens: Congregational Assets

The fourth approach to understanding your congregation's situation has to do with resources available for the life and mission of the congregation—human resources, finances, commitment levels, reputations, facilities, and others. Explore your congregation's resources by leading a group through some of the following exercises: membership demographics, survey of facilities, the budget, and commitment.

MEMBERSHIP DEMOGRAPHICS

If your congregation annually compiles statistical data about members (ages, gender, membership, worship attendance, baptisms, giving levels, and so forth), invite the group to review this information from a five-to-ten-year period. Some denominations compile such data and publish it on the denomination's website. Members of the study group can add their own general impressions about the educational and income levels of members. What trends, if any, are found in these demographics? How do they compare to the demographics of the church's neighborhood?

SURVEY OF FACILITIES

Conduct a review of your church building, and then discuss what your findings say about the congregation and its mission. What does the architecture of the sanctuary suggest about the congregation's theology of worship? Can visitors easily find their way to the church offices, sanctuary, and other key locations? Are your buildings accessible for people with disabilities? What would make your buildings more accessible to visitors and people with disabilities? How well are the facilities maintained, and who maintains them? Is the size of the facility appropriate for the congregation today? Who uses the facilities on a regular basis? Are neighbors welcome to use church space for community activities of any kind? Why or why not?

THE BUDGET

Look closely at your congregation's current annual budget. What does it communicate as a theological statement? What does it say about the congregation's values? If records are available, look at the level of giving by different age groups. What do your findings suggest about the ways different generations understand their commitments to the church?

COMMITMENT

Invite your study team to make a list on newsprint of generally held expectations of members—for example, attending worship regularly, making an annual pledge, participating in Christian education events, serving on a church committee, helping with community ministry, and so forth. After the list is compiled, ask them to rank order these expectations. Discuss how the top-ranked expectations are lived out by members. What confusion might exist about these expectations?

While many of these suggested exercises have a sociological dimension, they are also deeply theological. They pose critical questions about the nature of God at work in the world and about the vocation of your congregation. These exercises provide ways for the people of God to explore their collective situation, to look for signs of God's presence, and to discern new ways that God is calling the church to renewed faithfulness.

The Congregation's Lay Committee

If theological education is best done by the whole church—not just the ordained clergy or trained theologians—it follows that any teaching congregation would call a team of laypeople to commit themselves to working with pastoral interns, engaging in routine theological reflections and vocational formation. It is quite unrealistic to expect that theological students can be prepared adequately for pastoral leadership simply by attending classes and apprenticing with a pastor. Laypeople who accept this call to service are performing a critical service to the larger church in the education of men and women for ministry.

Ideally, service on the committee is as valuable to lay members of the team as the committee is to the student. As laity engage a pastoral intern in understanding his or her vocation, it is hoped that they will also examine the claims of the gospel upon their own vocation; and as they explore theological convictions expressed in the intern's practices, it is hoped that they will grow in their own theological understandings.

GUIDELINES FOR ESTABLISHING THE COMMITTEE

Nothing is more frustrating to active and committed laypeople than to serve on a congregational committee that has no sense of purpose or direction. So to assist supervisor-mentors and interns to establish a lay committee for theological field education, the following guidelines may help clarify ways the team might work with an intern.

PURPOSES

The congregation's lay committee has three basic purposes: (1) to extend support and hospitality to the intern, assisting him or her to enter fully into the congregation's life; (2) to provide feedback and assessment for the intern, including reflecting together on specific events in the intern's ministry; and (3) to engage in theological reflections with the intern about the life and mission of the congregation.

SELECTING THE COMMITTEE

Normally the supervising pastor-mentor is responsible for enlisting people to serve on the team, with the governing body of the congregation confirming their appointments. The optimal size of the group is four to seven members who represent a broad cross section of the congregation. Those asked to serve should be people who understand their own vocation as an expression of Christian ministry, are involved in and understand the congregation, are open to sharing about their own life and hearing the story of others, and enjoy a shared approach to learning.

Committee Leadership. The supervising pastor-mentor should appoint a moderator who is skillful in group processes and can keep a group focused. Neither the pastor nor the intern should serve as moderator. An effective moderator frequently makes the difference between whether your committee accomplishes its stated purposes or simply wanders aimlessly. To ensure that committee meetings promote theological and spiritual growth, the moderator and intern will do well to consult with each other before each meeting to agree upon an agenda and a process to be used.

Role of Supervisor-Mentor. The supervising pastor-mentor may use the contents of this chapter to train and organize the group for its work. Beyond that, he or she normally serves as a general resource person for the committee. He or she is welcome—but not required—to attend committee meetings. One of the most important roles of the supervisor-mentor is to communicate to the team a sense of enthusiasm for their work.

Frequency of Meetings. Committees that meet too infrequently run the risk of never developing trust or mutual accountability. Normally, if the intern is serving for nine to twelve months (full time or part time), the committee should meet at least monthly. If the intern is doing a full-time summer internship, the committee should meet at least every two weeks.

Confidentiality. From the outset, the intern and committee must enter into a covenant of confidentiality. Because of the sensitive nature of information shared by participants, compromising this code can lead to pain and embarrassment that is contrary to the spirit of theological discernment.

A SUGGESTED AGENDA FOR THE COMMITTEE

Once the committee is selected and leadership roles are clearly defined, the committee members and the intern will need to establish how they will proceed with the nitty-gritty of their work. The following is a suggested step-by-step process that includes a preliminary time for getting organized, an initial meeting with the intern for relationship-building, routine gatherings throughout the internship for theological reflection, and a concluding evaluation process.

THE ORGANIZATIONAL MEETING

Prior to the intern's arrival, the committee meets with the supervisor-mentor for training and organizing. This includes ensuring that committee members clearly understand the purposes of the committee; getting to know one another better; identifying what your congregation can offer to the intern, as well as what the congregation can realistically expect from the intern; making plans to welcome the intern; and scheduling the first meeting with the intern.

INITIAL MEETING WITH INTERN

Soon after the intern arrives, preferably in the first week of the internship, the team reconvenes for an initial meeting with the intern. After introductions, you might begin by asking the intern to tell about his or her journey of faith, and then use the "Congregational Timeline" exercise on page 80 to tell the story of the congregation. End the meeting by establishing a schedule of future dates and praying for the work of the intern and committee.

ONGOING MEETINGS THROUGHOUT THE INTERNSHIP

Subsequent sessions, scheduled at regular intervals throughout the internship, either examine a pastoral event in the intern's ministry *or* examine some aspect of the life and mission of the congregation. The basic intent of both options is to engage in a process of shared ministerial reflection.

If the session focuses on the *student's practices*, the student should prepare a brief written document and distribute it a few days in advance to the committee. The document might be a sermon manuscript, a lesson plan, a case study, or a review of a critical incident in ministry. A typical meeting might proceed something like this:

1. The intern presents the written report and clarifies anything that is not clear.
2. The group probes the significance of the event for the intern, especially any emotional response that the intern had during the incident.

3. Committee members share occasions in their own lives in which they experienced similar feelings or issues.
4. The team and intern identify and explore biblical texts or confessional documents that speak to the incident.
5. The team and the intern identify implications: What solutions or changes need to be considered from the study of scriptures and creeds?[16]

If the agenda of a session focuses on *congregational practices*, the intern and moderator might select some of the exercises from congregational studies that explore the culture, context, processes, or resources of the congregation.

FINAL MEETING

The final meeting of the committee is a time for an assessment of both the pastoral intern *and* the congregation's intern program. The intern's school normally provides an instrument for assessing the student's work throughout the internship. For assessing the congregation's performance in the program, the following questions may be helpful:

How have we helped or hindered this intern in achieving his or her learning goals?

How effective were we in providing effective feedback to the intern?

How effective were we in looking honestly at the life and witness of our congregation?

What changes should we make with future interns?

What have been our personal learnings and disappointments from serving on this committee?

Generative Congregations

Although it is generally believed that the single most critical variable in the quality of any pastoral internship is the supervising pastor-mentor, some congregations seem to provide distinctly generative experiences for theological students year after year, even when a pastoral leadership transition occurs. These congregations apparently have an inherent capacity to guide pastoral interns along the road to faithful leadership in the church. There is something about their ethos that teaches. But what?

In a study of several teaching congregations, theological field educators from several seminaries identified congregations that they saw as being particularly generative for theological field education. Through on-site studies, fourteen discernible *habits and virtues* were identified that distinguished them. These traits are summarized and grouped under the four lenses for congregational studies.[17]

CULTURE—THE IDENTITY OF GENERATIVE CONGREGATIONS

Generative congregations have a culture that is future oriented, theologically grounded, missionally focused, and worship centered.

1. *Future oriented.* Generative congregations know and appreciate their history but are not enslaved by it. Most have had past seasons of glory as well as times of struggle, but they are not trying to return to the good old days. Instead, they see themselves as communities of hope guided by a positive vision of the future.
2. *Theologically grounded.* Generative congregations are guided by theological discernment in making decisions and dealing with change. This is not to suggest that they see themselves as "great theologians," but they do see the biblical witness as a critical guide for life and mission. They see God as deeply engaged in the world, concerned not only about the hereafter but also with the quality of human life.

3. *Missionally focused.* Generative congregations focus their energy on mission, not on their own survival. They are able to articulate a sense of mission beyond themselves, especially with people in need.
4. *Worship centered.* Generative congregations affirm that the worship of God is central to their sense of purpose and identity.

ECOLOGY—THE GENERATIVE CONGREGATION IN CONTEXT

The generative congregation is contextually savvy, publicly engaged, and cooperatively linked.

5. *Contextually savvy.* Generative congregations have a working knowledge of their local and world context. They are aware of the needs of their neighbors and the community's assets, and they plan for mission in light of these factors.
6. *Publicly engaged.* Generative congregations seek to promote the public welfare of their community. Social justice and civic involvement are cherished values. They often make their facilities available to community organizations and see themselves as good citizens.
7. *Cooperatively linked.* Generative congregations promote active partnerships with other agencies and faith communities to achieve common goals. They acknowledge that they cannot achieve their mission goals alone, so they partner with others who share common cause.

PROCESS—THE DYNAMICS OF THE GENERATIVE CONGREGATION'S LIFE

Generative congregations demonstrate shared leadership, are hospitable, and are grace-fully managed.

8. *Shared leadership.* Generative congregations embrace the value of lay leadership and empower both clergy and laity for

ministry. They affirm a variety of gifts for ministry, not just those of ordained clergy. Although enlisting people for mission is sometimes a challenge, they eventually find enough people to assume leadership roles.
9. *Personally hospitable.* Generative congregations readily welcome visitors and assimilate new members. Hospitality is a strong gift.
10. *Grace-fully managed.* Generative congregations make decisions and deal with conflicts in open, fair, and healthy ways. While they have conflicts, they see their disagreements as opportunities for growth.

RESOURCES—THE ASSETS OF THE GENERATIVE CONGREGATION

A generative congregation is programmatically balanced, focuses its resources on mission, has high levels of member participation, and is spiritually nurturing.

11. *Programmatically balanced.* Generative congregations are intentional about balancing worship, education, and fellowship with efforts in mission. They value the journey inward and the journey outward.
12. *Missional resources.* Generative congregations see their assets, including facilities and funds, as resources for the mission of God.
13. *Highly participatory.* Generative congregations expect and receive a high level of personal commitment and participation by members. They manifest an ethos of energy.
14. *Spiritually nurturing.* Generative congregations highly value their role in helping members grow in Christian faith and values. They are not concerned only with the Christian education of children and youth, but they emphasize spiritual nurture for all members. They educate not only for an authentic sense of personal piety but also for commitments to social justice and peace.

Although these generative qualities may suggest a somewhat utopian congregation, they are nevertheless important habits and virtues that can contribute significantly to the health of almost any congregation. It is rare that a congregation will exhibit all fourteen traits simultaneously, but they are helpful benchmarks that help define the character of strong teaching congregations.

More to the point of this chapter on congregations, these qualities can help the supervisor-mentor and lay committee to assess their capacity as a teaching congregation and to identify strengths on which to build for the future. An intern can use the list as guidance in finding a teaching congregation that will be a good fit for his or her theological education. Later, during the internship, the intern and lay committee together may use the list to clarify what vision of ministry is guiding their work.

A Few Concluding Words for Supervisor-Mentors

As a supervising pastor or mentor, one of your ongoing responsibilities is to provide timely and appropriate feedback to the intern. Indeed, feedback is a core function of theological field education. But as valuable as your personal feedback may be to the intern, there is much that the intern can learn by *also* receiving feedback from the laity of your congregation. Their perspectives richly supplement and reinforce the contributions you are making to the intern's ministerial formation.

In addition to carrying out this feedback function, lay members are uniquely positioned to interpret the life and mission of the congregation. After all, they are the real experts on the culture, processes, resources, and ecology of their congregation. They *are* the church. They are the people of God. Congregants may not always be of one mind about these matters, but even the variety of their views is instructive. So I urge you to take very seriously the great potential for theological insight that can come from interns and congregants working together to explore the ways that God is working among them. It is a win-win enterprise: *students* learn critical skills for serving a congregation, and *lay members* grow in their understanding of the mission of God. All grow in their capacities for theological reflection and missional service. Not surprising, a common outcome from lay involvement in theological field education is that the *people* of the congregation become increasingly excited about the value of reflecting together and growing in their capacity for mission. And interns who are fortunate to enter into such discussions are treated to an invaluable journey into theological education.

For all these reasons, I hope you as a supervising pastor-mentor will take very seriously your role with the lay committee. Enlist people for the job who can function at high levels. Train them carefully. Encourage them through your presence or by inquiring about their work. And pray for them. If you attend their meetings—and I hope you will occasionally—resist becoming the resident theologian who has all the "right" answers. Instead, frame questions that facilitate *their* discernment. Encourage team members and interns to critique unexamined theological assumptions and invite them to grow as disciples grounded in biblical texts and theological convictions.

Ministerial formation is not best understood as one generation of clergy handing off insights and traditions to the next generation of clergy. It is the work of the *whole* church. Theological discernment by clergy and laity *together* not only creates a generative context for theological field education but also defines a way for church members to grow in their common vocation as the people of God.

Concluding Words for Interns

I hope that you hear my enthusiasm for the rich opportunity for theological education that is available through doing supervised ministry in a congregational context. Congregations do not need to excel in all fourteen of the habits and virtues listed previously in order to be an excellent partner with you in your formation for ministry. In reality, very few congregations excel in *all* of these traits. And even if you were fortunate enough to find such a congregation, there is no guarantee you will have an outstanding experience with no problems. There are simply too many variables, including your own gifts and needs, *and* the chemistry between you and your supervisor-mentor. So don't waste energy trying to find the perfect congregation. Rather, look at your internship as a journey shared with a supervisor-mentor and a particular community of faith who offer particular gifts of hospitality, constructive feedback, and communal discernment about the mission of God.

When working with your lay committee to explore your own pastoral practices, take full advantage of this opportunity by becoming increasingly transparent about your feelings, by respecting (not to be confused with always *agreeing* with) the opinions of team members, and by expressing gratitude for their work. If you are seeking feedback on a pastoral encounter or critical incident, prepare for such meetings by writing out and distributing your reports of critical incidents to team members in advance. Not only will this help *you* to focus on what happened and to identify questions, but it will also allow them to provide much more constructive feedback. Of course, you can simply show up and tell everyone about something on your mind, but this seldom has the same results as when everyone prepares in advance.

When working with your lay committee to explore the situation of your teaching congregation, preparation is equally important. Work with your supervisor-mentor and with your committee moderator to identify an issue or dilemma that the congregation may be facing (or not facing), and then choose one or more reflective processes from the exercises described earlier in this chapter. Determine who will lead the meeting and collect needed resources for the discussion.

While it is true that the relationship between you and your supervisor-mentor may be the most critical variable in your internship, never underestimate the importance of learning together with a team of committed laypeople to discern what God may be doing among you. The internship *is* about you and your development, to be sure, but it is *also* about discerning and discovering the activity of God in the community of God's people. *This* is theological education at its finest. *This* is the forming work of the teaching congregation.

7
Self-Care and Community

JACO HAMMAN

You are on an exciting journey of formation and ministry. Through your field placement, you are involved in some form of ministry. Your journey has led you along many paths, and at this moment you are becoming a ministerial leader. The title for this chapter, "Self-Care and Community," is carefully chosen, for *self*-care needs much clarification.

The apostle Paul reminds us often that we are *members* of one body (Rom. 12, 1 Cor. 12, and Eph. 3). Thus we can imagine that there is no such person as a seminary or divinity school student or even a ministerial leader. No, there is only a student *with* her body, *with* his God, *with* her supervisor-mentor, *with* his counselor, *with* her spiritual director, *with* his congregation, and *with* her intimate partner, family, and friends. So too are relationships with society, culture, and the environment central to being formed into a ministerial leader who can serve God in a variety of settings. How we imagine leadership, for example, is influenced by corporate understandings of leadership. Also, the media floods us with images of what a healthy person would look like. Any conversation on self-care, however, raises our anxiety, for few of us have mastered the art of self-care. One tension we experience in self-care is that it takes commitment and we often feel we lack the time to concentrate on self-care. Another is that we need to do it ourselves, but we never have to do it alone. Asking, "Are you fit or unfit to be a pastor today?" Lloyd Rediger writes that "clergy fitness is a shared as well as a personal problem and responsibility."[1] A further tension intrinsic to self-care is that it is something you *do*, but it is also inherent in your *being*, who you are and who you are becoming.

Self-Care as a Theological Statement

As you engage in self-care, you make statements about your understanding of God and what it means to be created in the image of God.[2] Self-care can be defined as a *commitment to your optimal health and well-being for your own sake, for those who love and care about you, and in the service of God's kingdom*. Never promoting self-involved behavior or narcissism, self-care is one way to love yourself so that you can love your neighbor. Self-care

- is part of your salvation and sanctification, for Christ did not die only for your soul but also for your body (Gal. 2:20–21; Eph. 5:29);
- is a choice, an attitude, even before it becomes an act;
- is about awareness and focused attention on the messages your body sends you, for all self-care involves your body, whether directly or indirectly;
- is a form of stewardship, being faithful with the body God gave you;
- acknowledges that God created you as an integrated whole, a unit;
- is an undertaking that requires commitment;
- wards off physical, emotional, and spiritual sickness;
- asks that you confess and repent some of your life choices;
- becomes contagious, awakening self-care in others.

Your self-care needs to honor your multifaceted created nature as you seek ways to glorify God with all your heart, mind, and soul (Mark 12:30). Self-care is best imagined as many overlapping circles, each circle connecting with and affecting the other. Four primary areas of self-care, each addressing a core aspect of being human, are your physical, emotional and mental, spiritual, and relational self-care.

Physical Self-Care

The first step toward self-care is tending to these core aspects, beginning with the relationship you have with yourself as a body, for we are always embodied. It is to know what keeps your body vital, its longings and desires, its warts and wounds, its potential and its limitations. It is to be comfortable with your body's shape and sounds. The prophet Isaiah describes his call as the work of mourning, restoring justice, and rebuilding lives and cities in ruins. He begins this description by stating, "The Spirit of the Sovereign Lord is on me, because the Lord has anointed me to *preach* good news to the poor" (Isa. 61:1 NIV, emphasis added). Many of my students identify with Isaiah. Even though not all want to preach, the vast majority of students I have met want to know the right words to say in a given situation. Reading Isa. 61:1, we are at risk of thinking that ministry is about words. However, the Hebrew word we translate as "preach" is *basher* (stem: *bashar*), which literally means *meat* or *flesh*. Isaiah thus says, The Spirit of the Sovereign Lord is on [you], because the Lord has anointed [you] to *enflesh—to be*—good news to the poor.[3] God has called you to be someone to a neighbor or neighbors, to sisters and brothers in Christ. Enfleshment or embodiment requires mindfulness about self-care and the self you take into community.

Practicing physical self-care, at its most basic level, requires that you move your body and eat healthy foods. Moving our bodies does not come naturally to our sedentary lives. Here, we can follow our Lord Jesus, for one answer to the question, What would Jesus do? is: He would walk! Jesus walked along beaches, between towns, and on water. Walking many miles, he would tire (John 4:6). Walking is a practice in self-care. *How can you walk or move more?* Add to walking some strength training, healthy eating habits, and enough rest, and you have a rhythm that will sustain you in life. Congregational consultant and educator Roy Oswald quotes research that indicated that 94 percent of clergy between the ages of thirty-five and fifty had no defined physical fitness program; 78 percent were overweight by sixteen pounds or more; and 89 percent of the clergy polled admitted to poor eating habits.[4] Research by the Francis A. Schaeffer Institute of Church Leadership Development found "that over 70% of pastors are so stressed out and burned out that they regularly consider leaving the ministry." With more than a thousand pastors polled, 71 percent stated they battle depression.[5] *Where do you stand?*

Besides exercising and adopting healthy eating patterns, practicing physical self-care also demands that you pay attention to symptoms that might be related to stress and anxiety. Exploring the possible relationship between your migraine headache and something going against your grain (or will) can produce helpful insights. Likewise, discerning the potential relationship between being overweight, depressed, or anxious and emotions such as anger, loneliness, and frustration can bring new perspectives on how you manage your emotions and indicate possibilities of wellness.

As you integrate body, mind, and soul, your energy level and sense of vitality will increase, and stress-related and weight-related illnesses will decrease. You will discover that health is not defined by the absence of illness but by the presence of meaning. We find meaning in our relationship with God, in community with others, and as people called by God into ministry. This is grace, for it means that we can find meaning and discover health even when we are dying. Patients taught me this important distinction while I was a hospital chaplain to cancer patients and in a psychiatric hospital. Health defined by the presence of meaning, which we receive from

God Emmanuel, God with us, is grace. Support and encouragement from people around you and your sense of vocation can give you the motivation to commit to your self-care. This care includes emotional and mental self-care.

Emotional and Mental Self-Care

Emotional and mental self-care, as you can imagine, require different approaches. Emotional self-care is easier if you are comfortable with your own emotions and are able to share your emotions with words and not just by relying on your body language. Mental self-care speaks to being mindful of your thoughts and self-talk, especially the self-talk of your inner critic. When you are plagued with guilt feelings, feel insecure, worry, distrust people, cannot sustain intimacy, often find yourself angry, know shame intimately, are reminded by your inner critic of what a poor job your did, or hide trauma and pain deep in the recesses of your soul, you rarely are as effective in ministry as you could be. When you feel like a fraud, telling yourself that others will reject you if they discover your true nature, you will be defensive when confronted or challenged, seek perfection in preaching and teaching, remain inflexible when openness and change are required, or come across as arrogant or aloof. If your body is a temple, as Scripture teaches us, you need to be mindful of the emotions and thoughts that will make that tent their home (1 Cor. 6:19–20). Sharing your joys as well as concerns or past pain and future hopes with your supervisor-mentor, a spiritual director, or a counselor is practicing self-care within significant relationships.

By embracing your emotional life and by being mindful about your thoughts (Col. 3:2), you are like Moses, who was on the road to burnout until his father-in-law Jethro spoke up (Exod. 18). You minimize the risk of becoming like King Saul who developed a jealous eye, became enraged, and threw spears (1 Sam. 16). You grow in wisdom and spiritual authority, which Deborah (Judg. 4) and Timothy (1 and 2 Tim.) portrayed. And you emulate Priscilla, a coworker of Paul, who showed much courage (Rom. 16:3).

Spiritual Self-Care

Since God made you body, mind, and soul, caring for your spiritual self is integral to good self-care. Spiritual self-care beckons you to grow in God, to become more Christlike. As a theological student, you will read Scripture often and pray on a regular basis. The likelihood, however, is that you will read Scripture in an analytical way with an audience or specific assignment in mind. You will pray for others but rarely ask others to pray for you. Self-care requires that you read Scripture for yourself, that you often commune with God in prayer, and that you provide others with personal prayer requests. In addition, practice spiritual disciplines such as meditation, repentance, worship, or fasting.

Spiritual self-care must include taking a sabbath. Author Norman Wirzba writes that "sabbath is a discipline and practice in which we ask, consider, and answer the questions that will lead us into a complete and joyful life."[6] We align ourselves with God's life-building and life-strengthening ways when we take a sabbath. Finding a place where your body and soul can rest, where you can experience moments of solitude amidst the challenges of schedules, tests, papers, preaching, teaching, and practicing pastoral care, is crucial. Sabbath rest is also an important part of communing with God. Through spiritual self-care you open yourself to God's presence, deepen your relationship with Christ, and listen to the voice of the Spirit. Ultimately, spiritual self-care leads to a sacramental view of reality and honoring the sacred nature of life with a deep recognition that we live *coram Deo*, in the presence or before the face of God. Spiritual self-care mediates the Holy as our relationship with God deepens. Spiritual self-care imparts wisdom about good and evil and the relationship we can have with God through Christ. It nourishes new life within us but also between ourselves and others, building and reconstructing a sense of belonging and community. Also, spiritual self-care repairs the world for it brings hope to a world that knows despair. *What spiritual disciplines do you already engage in? And what disciplines can you adopt or explore, alone or with others?*

Relational Self-Care

In a virtual world of social networking where communication is reduced to abbreviated sentences, fleeting conversations, and "friends" whom we have never met, relational self-care is important. You are made into the image of the God who looks at you, who turns toward you so that you are face to face with God (Num. 6:24–26). Certainly, Facebook, Twitter, the next wave of social networking, or e-mail can be great resources to establish and maintain relationships, but they can also easily become time-consuming monsters leading to diminished self-care. One gift you receive as part of your theological education is that you have a supervisor-mentor and others who meet with you face to face. They incarnate Christ to you. As you grow in your self-care, surround yourself with many people who can look you in the eye, people who can hold you accountable for how you engage life and ministry. Build up "social capital," as pastor and educator Allison Moore writes, those "connections among individuals—social networks and the norms of reciprocity and trustworthiness that arise from them." She continues saying that "decreasing social capital diminishes both individuals and the society in which they live."[7] Your social capital increases when you build trust with people who care enough about you to ask difficult questions about your life and call. Such relationships empower you to stay connected in moments where conflict or tension wants to break the unity of Christ's body. The relationships allow you to be authentic and more than your role as student or intern or minister.[8] With increased social capital you can cultivate relationships with people who will care for you in times of need.

Overlapping Circles of Self-Care

As I said, I envision self-care as many layers of overlapping circles. Besides the areas already mentioned, I would like to briefly present two additional areas of self-care: sexual self-care and economic self-care. In my conversations with students, these two themes often surface with a sense of confusion and anxiety amidst a strong need to talk about these important facets of life.

Caring for yourself as a sexual being is confusing if the community one is part of has embraced a marriage ethic to address sexuality. A marriage ethic rarely encourages single people to nurture their sexual selves out of fear that it would awaken sexual desire and activity. Especially if you are a single person, you have discovered that you are left with powerful desires and many temptations but few ways to address them. As you extend self-care to your sexual self, discern carefully the *sexual ethic* that will guide your life and ministry. A sexual ethic speaks to any person, young or old, single or married. Embrace your own sexuality or sexual desires and resist the temptation of seeking fleeting gratification. Find additional ways, besides channeling sexual energy elsewhere, to address sexual desire, for such sublimation is a short-term coping mechanism and difficult to sustain over a long period of time. Rather, grow toward integration, which is "a process of making ever more sense of one's total experience of mind, body, and spirit."[9] Integration honestly faces and addresses sexuality in the total context of intimacy with self, others, and God. An integrated sexuality does not produce guilt feelings and it does not put you personally or the community at risk.

Another aspect of self-care is sound *economic self-care* and being a good steward of your material needs. Theological education is expensive and you may have to take out loans to cover some of your tuition and living expenses. Maybe you entered your present journey with significant college debt. I have witnessed students becoming extremely anxious near graduation and as they interview with congregations. Much of their anxiety stems from the fact that many congregations do not have a parsonage but expect their pastor to find housing that can be paid for with a modest housing allowance. Because their significant credit card debt came with records, these students stated they would not be able to secure a loan to buy a home. Sharing one's financial woes with a possible employer is difficult.

Finding healthy ways to engage your sexuality and engaging in sound stewardship are additional elements of one's self-care.

Live into Your Call

Being in seminary or divinity school, either you have received a call from God to the ministry or you are busy discerning what God's call for you might be. Regardless of whether you have a call or await one, I can imagine you anticipate a future seeking ways to live according to how you understand God's will for your life. Self-care, too, has some of its focus on the future and many years of living into your call. *To live into your call is to commit to a life and practices that can sustain you for years of service to Christ's body and in God's world.* You already started the process of living into your call by seeking further education and by engaging in self-care. When we no longer live into our call with intentionality, we put our calls, lives, and relationships at risk. Most of us know ministerial leaders who lost their calls, some through burnout and others by flaming out in some shame-filled scandal. Protect your call by practicing self-care and by seeking out a community that can be significant to you, as I mentioned in the paragraph on relational self-care.

The relationship between an individual and a community is beautifully described in my favorite African proverb: "My friends who love me grow on me like moss." In Africa and other parts of the world, mosses and lichens are often used for their medicinal qualities. The metaphor suggests someone is protected from the wounds of life or heals faster if friends and a community are part of that person's life. The support, care, and comfort we receive from others, but also the accountability they extend us, are life affirming. As Paul writes to the Corinthians, receiving comfort and compassion in community produces endurance and hope (2 Cor. 1:3–7). Imagine yourself covered in a blanket of soft, green, life-giving moss as core relationships with supervisor-mentors, family, friends, and God surround you with love and care. Sadly, most of us live by another proverb: "A rolling stone gathers no moss." We become rolling stones when we neglect our own self-care and isolate ourselves from a significant community. *By which proverb will you live?*

How to Enter into a Conversation about Self-Care and Community

Finally, to ensure that self-care is part of theological field education, I encourage the student, the field educator, and the supervisor-mentor to discuss self-care and to address the relationships that form the student's community. The questions below can guide your conversations.

BE ATTENTIVE TO PERSONAL AND INTERPERSONAL DYNAMICS

We pastoral types can be sensitive to criticism. A conversation about self-care can awaken many defenses in us, including but not limited to: anger ("Why are you bugging me about my health?"); denial ("Self-care is not an issue for me"); passive aggressiveness (the student does not show up for a scheduled appointment); somatization (a physical symptom appears); acting out with harmful behavior (such as binge eating, excessive drinking, or overspending); rationalization ("Between school and my part-time job, I have no time for self-care"); and even shame ("Look at my life. I am not good enough to be a ministerial leader. Maybe God did not call me to the ministry"). So too humor can be used in a defensive manner when we laugh *at* ourselves or others rather than *with* people ("At least I am not as fat as that one guy I saw on *The Biggest Loser*; he could not even see the scale!")[10]

Here I envisioned the defenses active in the life of a student, but the field educator or the supervisor-mentor too may not practice self-care. The field educator or the supervisor-mentor can be as defensive about self-care as the student is. Whether you are a student or a field educator or a mentor, engage these and other defenses as they enter into your supervisory relationship.

Most often, I envision, the field educator or mentor will introduce the topic of self-care. Ask what emotions or thoughts might hide behind behaviors and attitudes or whether a possible link exists between a recent conversation you had or planned to have and what is currently experienced. Be respectfully curious about any reactions to the conversation, and ask good questions that lead a student toward her or his strengths.

ASK THESE AND SIMILAR QUESTIONS

Below are examples of possible questions that can be asked by the field educator, the supervisor-mentor, or a student. As I stated, I imagine that most often the field educator or supervisor-mentor will introduce a general discussion about self-care and community, sometimes concurrent with a field education course addressing the importance of personal well-being in ministry. Of course, a student can also initiate the conversation and ask questions that will foster growth and new learning.

- Ask questions when engaging in self-care and being part of a community are not problems to be fixed:
  - When do you feel that you are engaged in really good self-care? Follow-up question: How can you create more moments like those in your life?
  - When do you feel most connected to a community that loves you and cares about you?
  - Describe a time in the past (week, month, year, ever) that you attended to your physical needs. Follow-up question: What can you do, even today, to have more moments like that in your life?
- Ask questions that externalize the concern:
  - How would your best friend or a close family member notice that you are engaging self-care and community at a deep level?
  - What do you think God would tell you about your self-care?

- What kind of community do you think God desires for you?
- How can your sense of call empower you to take self-care seriously?
- How can I pray for your self-care and community needs?
- Ask questions about recent changes:
  - What is different in your self-care (or experience of community) this week?
  - How are you moving your body (or resting) differently compared to last week?
- Ask questions that take the student into the future:
  - With regard to your self-care, where would you like to be five years from now?
  - Follow-up question: What are small steps you can take toward that vision?
- Ask coping questions:
  - How do you manage to not totally give up on self-care?
  - How do you stay connected to people as they encourage your formation for ministry?
- Ask self-interest questions:
  - What will you feel and think about yourself after a sustained period of self-care?
  - How will you grow personally and professionally if you are deeply connected to a life-giving and life-affirming community?
  - What kind of ministerial leader do you want to be?
- Ask scaling questions:
  - If ten is the best self-care and community you can experience and one is the worst, where do you plot yourself on this scale today? Follow-up question: What can you do to move up just one notch on this scale?

Do change the questions as each overlapping circle of self-care and community is explored. The answers the student provides will offer additional material to continue the conversation.

An Ongoing Journey of Self-Care

In these few pages, I certainly did not exhaust the possibilities of self-care. As you the student intern grow in self-awareness and as you converse with your supervisor-mentor, you will discover additional aspects of your self-care journey. Do empower yourself to make self-care and community part of your life vision as well as your call.[11] Receive God's grace anew every day as you engage in this important task of your formation and ministry. God, who called you into this journey of theological education, is with you, face to face, as you embrace your own self-care in the community God placed around you.

8
Ministerial Ethics

BARBARA BLODGETT

Why a chapter on ethics? Surely writing to ministers in training about morality is redundant. You wouldn't be in seminary if you weren't a good person, right? So why do you need someone to tell you how to conduct yourself in your field education internship? Aren't the ethics just implied in what you are doing?

Not as much attention has been paid to the ethics of ministry as to the ethics of other professions and vocations. Medical ethics, business ethics, legal ethics—these and other kinds of ethics are well-formulated disciplines about which much has been written and lively debates carried out. But ministry ethics—well, it seems that few people see the need. Unfortunately, the one thing that draws attention to ethics in the ministry is scandal. When ministers make the headlines for abusing their congregants or embezzling funds or concealing immoral lifestyles, then a cry goes up for ministers to become more ethical. Insurance companies get involved, policies and procedures are drawn up, and rules and codes are established. These reactions are entirely understandable and appropriate, of course, because innocent and trusting individuals who are hurt by a minister's behavior deserve redress. But my point is that inattention to ethics is a deeper problem that goes beyond the scandals and the obvious wrongs of misconduct. The church would be better served if all of us gave more thought to the kind of people and communities we ought to be.

Ethics, after all, is not just about figuring out the rules of right and wrong but also about identifying the habits and practices that shape our character as individuals and communities and make us the best we can be. Let me briefly name three reasons, therefore, why ethics is important to ministry in general before we talk about field education in particular. First, the moral habits of individuals in ministry have never been more important. According to the annual Gallup poll that ranks professions in terms of Americans' trust, attitudes toward clergy have fallen over the years. In 2009, they slipped into eighth place for trustworthiness, below other professionals like nurses, pharmacists, and elementary school teachers. Though a poll like this obviously needs to be interpreted, it does reveal that as a group, ministers cannot assume the level of trust in society that they once enjoyed. But I believe that for people in the pews (if not Americans at large), there still exists a deep yearning for ministers who are trustworthy. Congregants want in their pastors and priests strong and reliable leaders. They are willing to risk being open and even vulnerable with each other and look to ministers to lead the way. They do not so much demand a model of perfection but rather a responsible use of power and authority that respects the trust pastors and priests are given. In short, people in the church deeply desire from their ministers effective and authentic ministry they can trust. This is the first reason ethics is important.

I believe a second reason is that for their own part, ministers themselves want to be more trustworthy. They know they can no longer just take people's trust in them for granted and so they, too, strive for effectiveness and accountability in their ministry. While some ministers might like the freedom to do whatever they want and write their own rules, the vast majority actually want to be held to expectations shared within their faith community. In fact, some are dismayed to find that the level of accountability in ministry is not what they expected. When ethicist Richard Gula published his book *Ethics in Pastoral Ministry*, he explained that one of the reasons he was prompted to write it was the disappointment expressed by several of his colleagues that ethical standards seemed so unimportant in their profession. Those entering ministry after a career in another profession were especially surprised to discover that they would receive no performance reviews or evaluations, and their church had no code of ethics. These were not individuals who were floundering or confused about morality but rather ones who set high standards for themselves and associated high standards with respect. Their dismay suggested to Gula that a perceived failure to expect excellence of priests might be one reason for lack of morale in the priesthood.[1] After all, if no one cares, why bother? If no one entrusts you with real things, why work so hard to be trustworthy? Therefore, attention to ethics in ministry is important because it signals that ministry *itself* is important, and deserves to be done with excellence and concern for being the best possible minister one can be.

A third reason I would offer for the importance of ministry ethics is that people have a deep desire to see the church be the church. By this I mean that people who go to church seek something there that they cannot find in the rest of their lives. Quickly receding are the days when people go to church merely out of custom or social expectation. All the talk of today's Christians being spiritual but not religious obscures the fact that people are still turning up at the doors of religious institutions. And what they are looking for in those institutions, beyond a sheer sense of belonging, is a trustworthy and authentic community. They want a place where they can grow in their faith and practice it with others. In other words, people today are seeking practices of spirituality within a community they trust. Therefore it becomes all the more crucial that our communities of faith be places where people in the community can entrust themselves to each other, not just to pastors.

Covenantal Ethics

There are many principles upon which to ground a discussion of ministry ethics. For the purposes of this chapter, I choose the principle of *covenant*: the minister's relationship to people is best understood as a covenantal one. Not only does the concept of covenant undergird the trust I believe is necessary in ministry today but it is also apt for field education, because a field education experience lies at the intersection of several trust relationships (among school, site, and intern). Field education, to put it simply, is all about covenants.

What does it mean to say that a relationship is a covenantal one? *Covenant* describes both the way a relationship gets established and the type of relationship itself. We often think of covenants as the promises, contracts, or agreements we make with others; therefore, at its simplest, a covenantal relationship is one where we strive to live according to the promises we have made with one another. But a covenant has special features that distinguish it even from other kinds of promises, agreements, and contracts. We can look to the biblical narrative about covenant to inform our understanding of human covenant making in general and ministerial covenants in particular.

In the stories of Noah, Abraham, Moses, and David, we see a gracious and loving God covenanting to form an everlasting relationship with God's people (Genesis 9, Genesis 17, Deuteronomy 5, and 2 Samuel 7, respectively). What features of covenant can we draw from the biblical tradition? First, we see God establishing covenant out of pure gratuity. God is not motivated by anything the people have done but rather spontaneously reaches out and initiates a relationship on God's own. In Gen. 17:8 we hear God simply announcing to Abraham (about the generations to come of Abraham's offspring): "I will be their God." Period. God's statement is a straightforward, unmotivated declaration that forms relationship. Properly speaking, we don't *deserve* the covenant God makes with us. As Gula puts it, "The basic feature of the covenant is the very way it is formed; namely, grace is the first move."[2]

In establishing covenant, God makes promises with Noah, Abraham, Moses, and David that are explicitly binding and everlasting. There is no suggestion that God will revoke the covenant at a later date if God is not satisfied with the outcome. While the Sinai covenant story details a list of commandments God expects the people to uphold, the context of even this covenant is a gracious gift extended by a God who has delivered the people out of bondage as promised. In other words, the biblical tradition consistently presents God's covenantal relationship as irrevocable, not contingent upon human response. Another way of saying this is that the divine covenant is based not on the idea of a tit-for-tat exchange but rather, as ethicist Joseph L. Allen puts it, on God's "dependable graciousness."[3] At the same time, however, the biblical tradition does suggest that some response on the part of the people is always hoped for. While humans can never respond in kind to God's extraordinary gift, it could be said that there is at least some understanding of reciprocity to the divine covenant. Indeed, it could be argued that a covenant God initiates is never truly brought to completion without some sort of human response. It is a gift offered graciously and without expectation, but like other gifts, its true fulfillment requires human acknowledgment and enjoyment of it. Thus built into the idea of covenant is the additional notion of openness to an outcome as yet unknown.

This leads to another feature of covenant according to the biblical tradition—the acceptance of *risk*. The people of Israel have to take enormous risks to accept the covenant God extends. Even though God assures Noah, for example, that a flood will never again destroy the earth (Gen. 9:11), and Abraham that he will become the father of many generations (Genesis 17), it is no easy thing for people to entrust themselves to such promises. Indeed, Abraham's first response to God's declaration was to fall on his face and laugh (Gen. 17:17)! It could even be argued that God, too, takes a risk on the people of Israel, not knowing entirely whether they will honor and fulfill the covenant. Indeed, the biblical witness shows that God's relationship with the people Israel took different shapes throughout history. Entering a covenantal relationship always involves risk. A covenant is unlike a contract in this regard. It does not carry stipulations and details. Covenantal relationships are characterized by openness and have unpredictability built into them. In a covenant, both parties extend themselves toward the other under conditions of uncertainty. They make themselves vulnerable to each other.

Covenants are formed when parties to the relationship *entrust* themselves to each other and let themselves be trusted in return. Trust always involves some measure of vulnerability and risk, as we put ourselves in another's hands without knowing for sure how they will act. Part of what we entrust them with is, in fact, the *discretion* to act with our best interests in mind. But discretion, by definition, cannot be detailed in advance. This makes covenantal relationships an expression of faith, of openness, and of hope in things unseen.

Another feature of the divine covenant is its openness to all. Particularly in the Noah story, we see God forming an inclusive covenant: the whole human community, indeed, all living creatures, are included. "I will remember my covenant that is between me and you and every living creature of all flesh" (Gen. 9:15). Without necessarily settling the theological debate as to whether God's covenant extended just to the descendants of Israel or universally to all humans, we can affirm that a spirit of inclusivity characterizes covenantal relationships in the biblical tradition. Covenants may be made between particular parties, but they do not thereby involve any sort of favoritism or the creation of an in-group and an out-group. Covenants are not formed to include some at the expense of others.

A final feature of covenant should be mentioned. Sometimes covenants are formed between parties that are equal in status and power, but not always. Obviously, humans are not equal to God, and this proves that sometimes one covenantal partner may have more power than the other. In such a case, risk and vulnerability are disproportionately shared. This means that the party with more power must assume a greater share of responsibility for the relationship.

From these features of divine covenant—gracious, involving risk, embracing openness, and requiring responsibility—flow the features of human covenantal relationships. The biblical covenant tradition, in other words, sheds light on covenant making among people of faith and can provide the basis for the ethics of their relationships, including ministerial relationships. To model ministerial relationships on the biblical covenant tradition, means, first, that we do not serve people because they have deserved it. We don't minister only to those we prefer or find attractive, but rather we serve all. While ministers (including interns) serve particular communities, often out of choice, they do not single out some people for more attention than others. In the ministerial relationship, all people are the same; covenantal relationships are inclusive and gracious, not exclusive and self-serving. The ministerial relationship also acknowledges the vulnerability of those served and the risky business that being ministered to entails. Ministers should always seek to minimize others' risk by respecting them and not exploiting their trust. Finally, ministers must acknowledge the disproportionate power they have in the ministerial relationship and aim to balance it by taking responsibility for the relationship.

Covenants in Field Education

I said earlier that field education is all about covenants. A field education internship represents a covenant among three parties: the school, the intern, and the supervisor-mentor (four, if you include the site itself as a party separate from the supervisor-mentor). In the program I administered, the Learning Agreement form had a space at the bottom for three signatures: the student's, the supervisor-mentor's, and mine. No internship could go forward without those three signatures, not only because I was a stickler for details but also because I took the covenantal nature of field education seriously. One point of gathering all three signatures was that they became the sign that sealed our relationship going forward and reminded us of our promises.

Three signatures also signal to us that in field education, agreements are made among three parties. Most of the time we are used to thinking in terms of two-way covenantal relationships; therefore, one of the central ethical challenges of field education is honoring a three-way covenant. Let me give some examples of how tricky but important this can be.

Imagine that because he felt deeply loyal to his supervisor-mentor, an intern has not yet informed the theological field educator of conflict in his congregation that is escalating and putting him (and possibly the school) in an untenable situation. He thinks that loyalty means not airing the congregation's dirty laundry. Or imagine a supervisor-mentor who grows increasingly committed to and grateful for her intern. She accedes to her intern's request late in the semester to extend the internship beyond the time frame they originally agreed to. In both cases, the individuals' motives might very well be unblameworthy and even admirable, but there are still limits on what an intern and a supervisor-mentor can agree to on their own without involving the field educator. After all, their relationships are made possible in the first place because of covenants they both made with the school.

Other examples: Imagine that out of frustration with her supervisor-mentor, an intern shared gossip about him in her weekly peer reflection group that subsequently got leaked to the student who was interviewing to be his intern the following year. Imagine a field educator who wanted to do a particular supervisor-mentor a favor because he needed her influence in another context, so he made an exception for her intern that he didn't make for any of the others that year. In these cases, the behavior at hand (gossip, seeking influence) is ethically questionable on separate grounds, but the point is that in each case, one of the parties to the covenant is overlooked. In the instance of the frustrated and gossipy intern, the school is essentially the forgotten third party along with all of the other potential interns at the school who may be affected by what she said. In the case of the field educator who made an exception, other interns as well as supervisor-mentors participating in the program that year were potentially treated unfairly. In other words, when covenants are complex and involve more than just two parties, the ripple effect on other parties can be wide. In my experience in field education, unintentional and even well-meaning actions on one person's part could jeopardize quite a number of others.

These particular examples may not seem to you to represent huge ethical problems, but I highlight the challenges of honoring three-way covenants in field education because, in fact, they are not unique to field education. They arise in ministry all the time. (Dilemmas around confidentiality, in particular, often raise the question of which covenant a pastor should honor.) In fact, many of the dilemmas of ministry arise precisely because a minister is in covenantal relationship with several people at once. A pastor of a congregation, for example, must honor not only the relationships she has with individual congregants but also those with her congregation as a whole, and indeed, with her denomination and the wider church. Pastors working in multistaff congregations, not to mention other kinds of ministers working in agencies and organizations, frequently negotiate multiple relationships at once. Sometimes the obligations of these various covenants conflict with each other and the minister must make difficult choices. Therefore, the three-way covenants of field education are not unusual but represent a foretaste of things to come. Learning to honor them as an intern will be good practice for you.

Ethical Issues in Field Education

On the first day of every new academic year, I used to give a lecture to the new interns on the ethics of being an intern. In seeking a way to make my points both pithy and memorable, I started calling my lecture "Three Things You Should Not Accept at Your Internship." The three things were secrets, sex, and money. I did not then, nor do I now, wish to make light of the ethics of confidentiality, personal relationships, or gift giving, but I do believe that in order to honor the covenants involved in internships, interns should not become recipients of these things. Let us take each issue in turn.

SECRETS

There is great power attached to hearing a secret. When another person takes you into her confidence, they are often taking a risk and making themselves vulnerable to you, especially if the information reveals something significant and personal about them. To be privy to a secret, then, is to be entrusted. In fact, the etymological root of the word *confidence* makes the connection: the Latin verb *fidere* means "to trust." We become, in effect, trustees of other people's information when we hear their secrets and promise to keep them. Some people like to claim that the word *secret* implies a nefarious interaction while a *confidence* is by definition a good thing, but I simply understand confidentiality to be hearing a secret from someone and promising to keep silent. Just like any other secrets, some confidences are good and some are bad. In any event, becoming entrusted puts us in a position of power.

It can be quite seductive, therefore, to become someone's confidant. For an intern, having someone in the congregation where you are interning tell you a secret can make you feel like a bona fide member of the clergy. Acknowledging this seduction is important. Interns are sometimes treated as players with too little significance, so discovering that you are considered approachable and trustworthy can be a nice affirmation of you and your role. But the feeling of power should not be enjoyed at the expense of doing the right thing with the secret. Sometimes clergy these days sense that they have fewer and fewer occasions when they are powerful. As I have written elsewhere, "One of the 'sexy' moments in the ministry (of which there are precious few) is getting to say, 'I can't tell you that; it's confidential.'"[4] But this isn't an excuse for promising absolute silence.

What *is* the right thing to do when you are asked to keep silent? Many clergy and laypeople alike remain confused about the laws and ethics of confidentiality in the ministry. A lot of people seem to think that anything told to a minister is confidential, regardless of the circumstance, and some think the courts back up this view. Upon reflection, they might acknowledge that a remark made to the pastor in the produce aisle at Kroger hardly counts as a confidence, but they still harbor an inflated notion of what a pastor can keep confidential. Ethicist (and field educator) Joseph Bush calls this "the popular perspective's elevation of confidentiality."[5] Just to be clear: while the laws vary from state to state, few courts would consider a pastor's right to confidentiality absolute, and the right to silence becomes even weaker in the case of Protestant clergy who lack the sacramental seal of a confessional. Moreover, most ministers are considered by their states to be "mandated reporters" who are obliged to report information they hear about abuse of minors and the elderly. While there persists a popular moral notion that all information told to a minister is privileged, this notion is not necessarily reflected in law.

A further factor operating in the minds of church people is that pastors are like therapists whose profession dictates that they keep their clients' secrets. But parish ministry both is and is not similar to mental health professions in this regard. Ministers promise confidentiality to those who seek their guidance and spiritual care for the same reason therapists do: to provide the assurance of safety that will allow people to unburden themselves. Because it can be very difficult to go talk to a member of the clergy, people must be able to count on the promise that what they say will not be repeated. Therefore, like therapists, ministers practice confidentiality in order to establish trust with those in their care. A pastor's counseling would not be competent without this trust. However, pastors differ from other professionals in that they covenant with people not just as solitary individuals or isolated "clients" but also as members of communities. The boundary is not drawn around two individuals alone, because they both belong to a larger pastoral community. As Gaylord Noyce wrote in his classic work on ministry ethics, "For the pastor, the 'client' cannot be made singular so easily as can the client for an attorney or a physician."[6] He was talking about cases in which a pastor hears a confidence from one member of a family that belongs to the church and the fact that therefore the entire family is under the pastor's care. But even if a member doesn't have family in the church, situations might occasionally arise when it would be a good and helpful thing for others on staff or in the congregation to be brought into the circle of confidence. The body of Christ cannot practice *its* healing and caregiving role if all members are treated as isolated individuals who relate to the pastor alone and don't know anything about each other. I am not trying to justify a pastor indiscriminately broadcasting people's sensitive secrets, of course, but rather recognizing that when it comes to the ethics of confidentiality, faith communities may have wisdom of their own beyond the practices of secular professions.

The ethics of ministerial confidentiality are complex and cannot be treated fully here. A few simple, hard-and-fast rules can be applied to all cases of hearing a secret. This is because a pastor's overall aim is to be trustworthy; doing whatever it takes to nurture trust is the fundamental ethical principle. Being entrusted involves exercising discretion. We don't want ministers to act robotically; we trust them to figure out what is best for us even if we don't yet know what that is. Sometimes it might even paradoxically be the case that trustworthiness means breaking a confidence. As ethicist Karen Lebacqz wrote many years ago in a book about ministry ethics built around a case of confidentiality, "To be trustworthy requires a kind of continuity both in breadth of actions and in depth that goes beyond individual acts of keeping confidence."[7] A covenant doesn't spell out all individual acts but involves using discretionary power.

My own view of the ethics of confidentiality in the ministry is that ministers should keep confidences once they have accepted them but should also try to work themselves out of the job of being the community's sole confidant. A covenantal ethic encourages pastors to nurture trust not just in themselves but also among the people, even if this means their taking some risks. I believe one important role the pastor of a congregation can play is to lead members toward entrusting *each other* with more information about themselves. One way covenantal relationships in the church can come to mean something is by congregants learning to listen to each other's stories, caring respectfully for the truths they reveal, and sharing each other's burdens.[8]

In any event, as an intern, you have a covenant with your supervisor-mentor that precedes any covenant of confidentiality with members of your internship community. You should not get in the way of relationships between congregants and their pastor and therefore should not promise to keep secrets from the pastor.

Sometimes people might try to *put* you in the way. (For example, they might tell you in private that a decision your supervisor-mentor made is unpopular in the community.) This is typically called *triangulation*. The term suggests one person avoiding a second by going through a third. Needless to say, it is not a very healthy model of covenant. Triangulation seeks the easy way out; it avoids risk, when taking a little more risk would be better. Most of the time, it is best for all three people to be transparent with each other. Therefore, you should gently resist letting yourself be put in the middle and should make it clear that what you hear will also be heard by your supervisor-mentor. Situations may also arise in which you inadvertently come into important information. (Teens in the youth group, for example, might talk in front of you about drug use at parties that you don't think their parents know about.) You may have to remind would-be confiders that you cannot necessarily agree to keep the information to yourself.

Let me emphasize that when you decline to keep confidences as an intern, you shouldn't think of it as closing off a trust relationship but rather of facilitating an additional one. By helping people to share information more directly, you become the avenue for even greater openness and trust between them and their pastor. Most people are so used to thinking only in terms of closed, two-way promises of confidentiality that you might encounter some surprise when you suggest going to the third party, but you are modeling a different kind of covenant.[9]

Does honoring a covenant by sharing information mean that we no longer value privacy? Certainly not. All the aforementioned emphasis on openness notwithstanding, you should respect the privacy of people at your internship sites. Not *all* information has to be passed along. Do not share what people tell you without cause and certainly not without letting them know. Do not use the stories people tell you as sermon illustrations, for example, without their permission. Do not speculate on rumors or engage in gossip about people. Never run the risk of defaming or slandering anyone by repeating things you are unsure about. All of these behaviors violate covenant with people not only because they treat people as means to your own ends but also because they exploit the risk people took opening up to you. All individuals and their information should be respected.

You might have heard people in the ministry claim that drawing the line between gossip and pastoral conversation is difficult. Some even argue that to show care and concern for others in the community, you have to "gossip" about them a bit. Communities do vary in the degree to which members tacitly agree to share information about each other, and it may take time to get the feel for this in a community to which you are new. As an intern, err on the side of caution. Do not be the one to engage in talk that could appear salacious, that criticizes those not present, encourages conjecture about them, or treats their lives as entertainment. That constitutes gossip! The same guidelines hold true, incidentally, when talking about other supervisor-mentors in the field education program or other interns in your peer group.

Speaking of peer groups, let me add a word about them with regard to confidentiality. In many programs, peer reflection groups practice confidentiality in order to allow members to be able to talk freely about their internships. You might be asked to write cases based on your experiences, for example. If these are to be real rather than hypothetical cases, you will effectively be sharing information about people at your site "behind their back." You should therefore change names and disguise identifying details in your cases, and shred written cases once the discussion is over. More important, you should choose only to write about situations that shed significant light on ministry, not just dramatic or sensational cases that will impress your peers and make for lively discussion. Ultimately, your goal is to respect the people at your site by learning from your ministry among them.

A second reason for group confidentiality is that to engage in serious and intentional reflection on your ministries, group members need to be able to trust each other. Eventually you will want to share with your peers not only what is going on in your internship but also the ways your internship is challenging you. Most ministers who have been in the ministry for any length of time will tell you (*a*) that ministry is difficult, and (*b*) that the ability to be candid with one's peers about the difficulty of ministry is crucial. It makes the difference between a group that works and one that doesn't. Most seasoned ministers can tell a story about a peer group they quit going to after a while. When they suffer from a lack of candor, groups lack mutual trust, and when they lack trust, they merely become places to brag or to whine. The ministry does not benefit from braggarts or whiners, and neither will your reflection group. To make your groups safe and productive places for mutual sharing, then, many field educators will ask that you agree not to talk outside of class about what you learned about each other in class. (One exception might be to let the field educator into the circle of confidentiality when necessary.) Depending on the ethos of your school—where classrooms may or may not be considered confidential spaces—a practice of confidentiality in your peer group may be quite countercultural and take some getting used to. But it will become for you yet one more way to practice keeping covenant in the ministry.

SPECIAL RELATIONSHIPS

Most seminarians today have been taught the importance of boundaries in ministerial relationships, so you probably understand that you should not date anyone at your internship site. It is worth reviewing the reasoning behind this rule, however. There are two main ethical arguments against ministers having intimate relationships with members of their congregations, and these same arguments hold for interns. First, whenever a relationship is sexualized, an element of power goes along. Sex inevitably increases intensity. It stirs up feelings and emotions, not to mention beliefs about the self and others, that can be quite powerful. Some of these feelings are inevitably transferred onto the object of affection. But the relationship a minister has with people already involves an element of power. The minister is the more powerful party to this covenantal relationship.

To many people, their minister represents a special figure that they idealize and sometimes idolize. Few adults, perhaps, equate the minister *with* God, but she or he may constitute their connection *to* God and thus someone who possesses power to influence them. Therefore, to combine a pastoral relationship with an intimate one is to create the potential for a dangerous situation where power over the other might be exploited or abused. Congregants, moreover, deserve to have a pastor they can relate to just as pastor and are robbed of that chance when they get intimately involved, no matter how much they might desire the relationship. In keeping with the covenantal principle that the one with greater power bears the greater responsibility, the pastor therefore must ensure the freedom and safety of the congregant.

Ministers and congregants alike sometimes claim that they can handle being in both an intimate and pastoral relationship at the same time. This may be the case, but it is really beside the point. The second argument against intimate relationships in the ministry is that they constitute what ethicists call "special" relationships and, as such, inevitably favor some to the exclusion of others. If our covenants are meant to be as broad and inclusive as possible, then by selecting some people to be close to, we necessarily leave others out. By forming an inner circle, we inevitably create an outer one. Other people in the congregation are affected. Not only does their relationship to the pastor shift, as they perceive themselves to be less special, but the congregation also becomes a different place. In the case of sexual relationships, it is now a sexualized space and no longer promises to be a space safe and equally free for all.

The foregoing arguments are also relevant to close friendships. Whether a minister should make friends within the congregation is a tough question about which people hold different opinions. Some argue that it is simply human nature to prefer certain people over others and to become their friends. It can be particularly hard for a pastor, especially one who is single and new to the community, to make friends outside the congregation. But it is not necessarily easy to pull off friendships inside the congregation. One should never underestimate the privilege some people feel to have been singled out as the pastor's friend. Being close to the pastor may eventually become more of a burden on them than they initially realized. It may also become hard for the pastor to continue to pastor her friends and be able to preach to, teach, counsel, and admonish them.

You may be thinking that little of this applies to you as an intern who will, after all, spend only a year or two on site and probably part time at that. But the point is that as an intern, you are just stepping into the pastoral role. You don't have it all figured out yet; the demands of pastoring a congregation probably don't feel like second nature yet. All the more reason, then, not to try to juggle the additional task of trying to handle special relationships within your internship. It is in this light, incidentally, that you may be able to appreciate the policy your field educator has about not placing you in an internship where you already have family and friends or other kinds of special relationships. You deserve to learn the ropes of ministry in a context apart from those who already know you in these "special" ways.

MONEY

People probably won't attempt to slip you cash as an intern, so what I mean by *money* in this section is really gifts of monetary value, about which I believe interns should think twice before accepting. In my experience, interns are given a variety of gifts at their sites; these can range from free meals to liturgical garments to a place to live. Meals are perhaps the most common gift, and they are generally unproblematic. It is in fact a good sign when site members want to show hospitality to you. Problems may arise, however, if you are offered a gift of significant value, especially if it comes from only one person. The ethical principle operating here is that gifts can carry, or appear to carry, the expectation of a quid pro quo—something given or received for something else. If I give you this gift, you will be indebted to me and will pay me back in another way. Elected officials are not supposed to receive gifts from individuals or businesses that benefit from their votes, for example, based on this principle. In the church, an example might be the warden who offers you the use of his vacation home with the implicit or explicit expectation that you will support his proposals to the vestry. Nine times out of ten, no such expectation is intended, but even its appearance might trouble other vestry members. Again we refer to the theological notion of covenant: covenantal relationships embody mutual trust, not a quid pro quo. They are initiated out of grace with no expectation of return and, indeed, with openness to responses that might be totally unexpected.

I hasten to point out that church tradition varies greatly in practices of gift giving. In some cultures, gifting the pastor with material goods (beyond salary) is an honored practice of long standing. You would not want to offend anyone by refusing a gift if such a gift were traditional. The best thing to do is check with your supervisor-mentor. In general, I recommend the following guidelines: that interns receive only gifts given collectively by the entire congregation, and at the end of the internship rather than the beginning. Both guidelines underscore the gratuitous spirit of giving that is in keeping with a covenantal ethic.

In conclusion, how you learn to handle secrets, money, and sex in your internship is a clue to and foretaste of how you will handle covenantal relationships in general. By focusing on them, I point you toward your greater moral responsibility: to become a minister who is worthy of trust and who facilitates trust among the people you serve.

9

Language and Leadership

LORRAINE STE-MARIE

As you enter theological field education, you might find the language unfamiliar or different from what you have used and heard in other parts of your life. If so, take heart! You are in good company with many students who are new to theological or pastoral language. You are now in a learning environment that, like any other human organization, has its own language and language rules. In fact, every community—be it family, work or study settings, congregations, or even nation states—has its own language that shapes who people are, what we believe to be true, how we relate to others, and what we can and cannot do.

Robert Kegan and Lisa Lahey, developmental psychologists at the Harvard Graduate School of Education and coauthors of *How the Way We Talk Can Change the Way We Work*, make an important connection among leadership, community, and language. As researchers and practitioners in change leadership, they claim that every organization is a language community in which certain forms of speech are encouraged and other ways of talking are discouraged. Furthermore, they insist that all leaders—be they parents, CEOs, pastors, or national leaders—are actually leaders of language communities.

For them it is clear: Leaders can choose either to lead their language communities with intentionality and purpose or to mindlessly support whatever language the community prefers. And although every person in any organization can influence its language, "leaders have exponentially greater access and opportunity to shape, alter or ratify the existing language rules."[1]

I work in a Roman Catholic environment shaped by a theological language of church as a "community of disciples," which in turn forms students as they prepare for ordained and lay ministries. As a theological field educator who is cognizant of Kegan and Lahey's call to lead the learning environment as a language community, I intentionally use and encourage a language of *call, partnership, discipleship*, and *collaboration* as a way of consciously shaping their individual and collective identities as disciples. In my own experience, this language leads them to greater openness to seek out the gifts and wisdom of others in exercising their ministry.

How language communities shape seminarians and divinity school students can be seen in the work of Michael, a first-year ministry student, whose field education experience is used as an illustration throughout this chapter. Like many of us, Michael was formed in a family that had its own explicit language rules, one of which was that they had to talk nicely to each other even if they were really angry or hurt by one of their siblings. As Michael began to reflect on his experience of family as a language community, he came to see that the way he internalized that language rule shaped how he sees and relates to others. As you will see in this chapter, Michael's behaviors in his ministry were also implicitly shaped by this language rule.

This ancient Native American proverb also captures the spirit of theological field education: Tell me, I'll forget. Show me, I'll remember. Engage me and I'll understand.[2] Given the profound truth of this saying, I invite you to reflect on your own experience of family and to see what explicit or implicit language rules continue to influence you today. My hope is that this initial reflection might enable you to gain a greater understanding of how language affects yours and others' behaviors and the development of pastoral leaders.

Language and the Way We Think about Leadership

You have probably heard it said that language not only expresses our reality but also creates our *perception* of reality. There is an intrinsic relationship between how we think and what we do. Our language not only shapes how we think; it also influences how we feel about our particular experiences. In other words, the way we talk about our experiences affects how we think and feel about them, which in turn actually influences what we can do and cannot do.

Take a moment to think about some of your own experiences of leadership in a committee or team. In some instances, you might remember that although one person was exercising leadership through his or her formal authority, the leadership in that team changed when someone brought a different expertise or a clearer understanding to the issue at hand. On the other hand, you might recall some instances in which the leader with the formal authority clearly dominated the meeting and would not allow others to offer their expertise or points of view. These different experiences reflect different ways of thinking about leadership, which ultimately influences how we exercise our leadership.

If we take an entity-based approach to leadership—that is, if we think about leadership as being first the function of an individual—then we think of leaders and followers as entirely different people. Each has a distinct, fixed role. In this case, effective leaders have the right answer or solution, which they transmit to their followers to execute. There is a clear top-down delivery of information and expectations. In a process approach to leadership—that is, if we think about leadership as being a function of the relationship between leaders and followers—then part of being a good leader is being a good follower. In this view of leadership, effective leaders know the limits of their own ways of knowing and recognize that they need others' perspectives in order to gain a greater understanding of the problem before they implement a solution.

If we think of leadership as entity based, we keep a tight control on the dynamics in our environment to support our need to be right. However, if we think of leadership as process based, we open ourselves to other viewpoints by taking on both leader and follower roles, which mutually enrich each other. David Day, professor in the School of Business at the University of Western Australia, tells us, "Everyone needs to become a better leader in terms of being better prepared to participate in the process of leadership as the situation demands and as challenging events unfold."[3] This is one of the goals of theological field education: To prepare you to participate in the process of leadership. The program itself forms a language community, a space designed for you and your peers to transform and integrate the models and assumptions that shape your behaviors and delimit your choices. You will be given opportunities to try on different languages that have the capacity to release new energies and expand your ways of knowing.

Know that you are in good company with the ancient biblical character Jabez. According to 1 Chron. 4:10, "Jabez called on the God of Israel, saying, 'Oh that you would bless me and enlarge my border, and that your hand might be with me, and that you would keep me from harm!' And God granted what he asked." We cannot enlarge our borders without some change in our ways of seeing and acting. Be assured that just as God granted the ancient biblical character Jabez the security and confidence he needed to enlarge his borders, you too will be offered the support you need along the way.

The Language of Leadership Challenges

By now, you could be asking yourself, how much change and what kind of change will I be asked to live? The short answer is, it depends on the type of leadership challenges you encounter along the way. Ronald Heifetz, cofounder of the Center for Public Leadership in the John F. Kennedy School of Government at Harvard University, makes a distinction between two kinds of challenges that help us to understand and embrace two different kinds of change, not only in this program but also in the leadership roles you are preparing to take on. According to Heifetz, all of the challenges we encounter in our lives are either technical or adaptive.

Technical challenges are problems that can be solved from an existing body of knowledge and skills, whereas adaptive challenges take us into the unknown—there are no immediate, certain answers. To solve adaptive challenges, we usually need to change the way we think about that problem. This distinction helps us to see that we need to respond to technical challenges with technical solutions, and we need to respond to adaptive challenges with adaptive solutions.[4] While this formula seems quite simple and straightforward, in practice it can be much more complex and difficult to implement, because what could seem to you like a technical challenge (that has a simply clear solution) could also be an adaptive challenge, and vice versa. In addition, some problems are a hybrid of both adaptive and technical challenges and therefore require some existing knowledge and skills as well as changing the way we think about the problem itself. To probe these kinds of challenges a little further, let's join Michael in his field placement experience.

One of Michael's responsibilities in the congregation to which he was assigned was to lead the altar guild, a group of eight men and women. Three were fairly new to the community and five were long-standing members. Their mandate was to care for and prepare the altar and its furnishings. As part of his overall learning covenant, this assignment was designed to help Michael achieve his learning goal of developing his abilities for shared leadership. At first glance, it seems that leading this altar guild was a technical challenge, and part of it was. Michael needed to learn some things, such as what an altar guild does and does not do in this particular congregation. What are the general rules laid out by the denomination for what they do? What are the lines of communication between the altar guild, the worship committee, and the pastor? Who decides what, when, and how to do what needs to be done? These are all technical challenges that can be solved by accessing an existing repertoire of skills and knowledge. In addition, Michael also attended a training session on group dynamics to develop his competencies in group facilitation. Michael had changed in the sense that he had acquired more skills and information in order to meet what was in the first couple of months a technical challenge.

At the December meeting, a recurring agenda item—the cleaning of the sanctuary—provoked a very heated conversation that eventually turned into a shouting match between a longstanding member and a fairly new one. As their voices got louder, their choice of words became less and less polite. Although Michael tried to calm them down and encouraged them to speak nicely to each other, the meeting ended on a sour note. When everyone left, Michael sat for a while, shaken, wondering what he should have done differently. He called to mind his training in group dynamics, looking for clues about other ways he could have handled the conflict, yet in the end, he felt powerless and frustrated.

In raising this concern with his supervisor-mentor, he began to see that his skills training in group dynamics and conflict management was not enough to fix the problem. Rather than simply focus on fixing the problem of the conflict between two people, Michael was being called to focus on the meaning he had given to this and other conflictual situations in his own life. He was faced with an adaptive challenge. Michael's experience resembles the challenges that Heifetz says many leaders face today. It is difficult, if not impossible, to bring about the change we desire when we try to respond to an adaptive challenge with a technical solution.[5] The theological field experience is designed to offer you a space to work with both technical and adaptive challenges. With the support of your theological field educator and supervisor-mentor, you will discover that effectively responding to adaptive challenges often requires change in the way you understand or give meaning to the problem at hand.

The Language of Immunity to Change

Certain kinds of change are not easy, especially adaptive change that calls into question the meaning we give to our experience. Often we will associate people's inability to change with a stubbornness, hypocrisy, or just plain apathy. This may be true in some circumstances, particularly when change is imposed on us. However, as Kegan and Lahey tell us, this is not the case when we attempt to make a change to which we are truly committed. In their adult and leadership development research, they have discovered what they call a "hidden master motive" that keeps us at our current stage of meaning making.[6] Borrowing the term *immunity* from biology to explain what they found, they show us that all humans carry a hidden psychological dynamic of self-preservation that actually keeps us change-resistant. In this view, it is perfectly natural for all humans and human organizations to carry a simultaneous commitment to change and nonchange.

Just as our biological immune systems invisibly work at protecting us from illness or even death, our psychological immune systems also unconsciously protect us. However, at times we may need to disturb our biological immune systems with vaccines or medication in order to face new situations. For example, when I recently travelled to Haiti, I needed to have a polio vaccine and take malaria pills that would equip my body to respond to the new environment. The same is true for our psychological immune systems. At times we need to disturb our psychological equilibrium in order to meet the demands of new environments or situations.

Kegan and Lahey's "four column exercise" is designed to help us meet those demands by uncovering our hidden motivations and assumptions that keep us from making the very changes we want to make.[7] The objective of this exercise is to create your own personal mental map, a kind of X-ray of your meaning system, which anchors your immunity to change and keeps you from fully realizing the change to which you are committed. Each of the four columns has its own specific language in the form of questions designed to bring your hidden resistances to explicit awareness.

Michael's map in figure 9.1 (page 140) illustrates how to create your own mental map.[8] The power of the exercise lies in your working through it column by column. Therefore, I suggest you take a blank piece of paper to cover the whole map and then uncover one column at a time. If this is the first time you have encountered the four column immunity-to-change exercise, I strongly recommend that you work through it yourself. If you simply read how it works, you may find it interesting but you will miss an opportunity to experience the power of greater awareness of your own inclination

FIGURE 9.1: Michael's Four Column Exercise
copyright © Minds at Work

	1 LANGUAGE OF COMMITMENT	2 LANGUAGE OF PERSONAL RESPONSIBILITY	3 LANGUAGE OF COMPETING COMMITMENTS	4 LANGUAGE OF ASSUMPTIONS WE HOLD
	I am committed to ...	What am I doing or not doing?	I am also committed to...	If I ..., then ...
MICHAEL Develop skills of shared leadership – becoming better organized – developing better listening skills – acquiring greater confidence in dealing with conflict	– developing greater confidence in dealing with conflict.	I avoid speaking up when I don't agree with what is being said. I complain to others outside of the conflictual situation. I withdraw (either physically or internally) when conflict occurs. I try to minimize or quickly gloss over the conflict so that we can be at "peace."	Worry Box – loss of civility – loss of control – loss of respect for others and self – loss of positive regard by those who mean a lot to me – ensuring others see and know me as a person who is nice to everyone and does not take sides or support conflict.	*If* I do not ensure that others see me as a person who is nice to everyone and does not take sides or support conflict, *then* I will be seen as a troublemaker, and they will lose confidence in me. This could lead to my being rejected as a minister.

not to change. You will find a blank form for your personal work in figure 9.3 at the end of this chapter.

SHADED COLUMN: PRELIMINARY WORK

The shaded column in figure 9.3 is the warm-up step for naming the commitment you will put in the first column. If you have already created your learning goals for your theological field education experience, refer to them and ask yourself which of those goals are most important to you. If you have not, this could be a time to begin to consider what some of your learning goals will be this year. What goals are important to you? Now take a few moments to write them in the shaded column in the blank four column exercise. In figure 9.1, Michael has listed some learning goals. As you can see, he wants to develop his abilities in shared leadership. Under this broad category, he has named three specific areas for growth: becoming better organized, developing better listening skills, and acquiring greater confidence in dealing with conflict. All three of these specific learning goals are important to him and he is convinced that they will make a difference to his ministry if he makes some progress in achieving them. If you are following this exercise with your own learning goals, write them down in the shaded column before proceeding to column 1.

COLUMN 1: LANGUAGE OF COMMITMENT

The language of commitment is designed to transform your goals for change into genuine commitments.[9] This is done by looking at the goals you have written in the shaded column and then asking yourself the key question: To what goal am I truly committed but not yet fully realizing? In other words, what is the "one big thing" that I need to improve so that my ministry can flourish even more? Circle that one goal. Now, as you read what follows, you will quickly realize that this exercise cannot be completed in one sitting. If you want this exercise to give you the most mileage in your own growth, invite others into your plan. Consult with people who know you well enough to suggest which of your goals would be the most important for you to realize at this point in your ministry education. Then, ask yourself if you yourself are sincerely committed to realizing that goal. If not, the goal will not give you the energy needed to change.[10]

Let's look at Michael's map as an example. Michael did this exercise following the difficult situation with the altar guild. He consulted his supervisor-mentor, his field educator, and some of his peers with whom he had shared the issues and concerns in his leadership. While they all agreed that the three goals were important, they suggested that the one big thing that would make a difference for his ministry at this time would be "developing greater confidence in dealing with conflict." Although Michael had already sensed that this was where he was being called to focus his energy, it was good to have this confirmed by those who wanted the very best for him in his ministry education. What one big thing would make a difference to you? Write it down in your first column using the Language of Commitment, "I am committed to . . ."

COLUMN 2: LANGUAGE OF PERSONAL RESPONSIBILITY

In this column, we look at behaviors that are keeping us from *fully* realizing our first-column commitments. The key question for this column is this: "What am I doing or not doing that undermines or keeps me from *fully* realizing my first-column commitment?" I stress the word *fully*, because if you are truly committed to a particular goal, then it is quite likely that you are already doing a lot to support that commitment. Here the focus is on your concrete behaviors, rather than traits or attitudes. The goal of this column is to transform a generally more habitual language of blaming the other to a language of taking responsibility for our actions that work against our first-column commitment. But beware: it does not mean that we ourselves must take all the blame or try to fix the system in which we work or minister.

There are situations in which others have varying degrees of influence on our own behaviors. Moreover, some institutions and power relations leave people with very little or no choice about how they behave or act. However, this column makes explicit our capacity to take some (but not all) responsibility for our own actions that work against our most sincere commitment to change.[11] In some cases, self-disclosure and accepting our own share of responsibility is difficult. In fact, the way we respond to this second-column question can allow us to become even more conscious of the systemic forces in the larger context of our lives and ministry. And yet, we carry some responsibility for either maintaining the status quo or bringing about change. This awareness is important in ministry, where we could assume all the blame, simply blame the other, or claim powerlessness in the face of outer forces beyond our control. The "language of personal responsibility" shows us that we are powerless only to the extent that we are *unaware* of how our behaviors perpetuate the mentality we are committed to changing.

As you will see in Michael's map, his sincere commitment to increasing his ability to deal with conflict is being undermined by his own behaviors. Using the language of personal responsibility allows him to see that at times he avoids speaking up when he does not agree with what is being said and that he then complains to others outside of the conflictual situation. He also noted that he withdraws (either physically or internally) when conflict occurs and that he tries to minimize or quickly gloss over the conflict. It is important to note that in this column, you are not trying to explain why you are doing or not doing what you are doing. Rather, you are simply noting the behaviors themselves.

The fact that we do not practice what we preach is not a new discovery. That is true for all of us. However, it takes courage to name what we are doing that undermines our true commitment. Usually when we name our contradicting behaviors, we try to focus on either correcting or stopping them completely. Remember the distinction we made between adaptive and technical challenges? Trying to simply change our behaviors is a short-term technical solution to what is now beginning to look like an adaptive challenge. We all need to dig deeper to arrive at the source of our contradicting behaviors. If we do not, it is very likely that we will revert to our ineffective behaviors or worse yet, we will begin new ineffective behaviors. Even if we make some progress in reducing the second-column behaviors, these forces can hold us in a state of nonchange. The second-column work offers the opportunity to stretch and change our ways of thinking as we begin to notice the patterns of our behaviors.[12]

COLUMN 3: LANGUAGE OF COMPETING COMMITMENTS

This third-column language transforms our more habitual, quick-fix approach to change to one that recognizes we may actually hold commitments that give rise to the behaviors in column 2.[13] Kegan and Lahey call this the language of New Year's resolutions.[14] For many of us, change that comes from New Year's resolutions is usually superficial and short-lived. If we do not address our need for adaptive change, most of us resume our familiar habits and behaviors by the end of January.

Competing *commitments* are particular forms of self-protection that work against our first-column commitments. The questions in this column lead us to uncover our natural tendency to defend or protect ourselves from change, even the very change to which we are truly committed. The intent of this column is to make us aware of the contradiction between our true commitment and what it is we are actually doing. Psychologists say that when our existing beliefs or mindsets are challenged by new insights we experience a psychological tension that they call "dissonance." Our response to dissonance depends on a complex set of factors, including our temperaments and personal histories as well as the event or situation itself. In some cases, we might choose to avoid or ignore the psychological tension and in other cases work with it. Studies have shown that one of the factors in determining whether dissonance will lead to change is the degree of personal responsibility we take for our actions.[15] The more personal responsibility we take for our behaviors, the greater the possibility of transformation. Therefore, if we are truly committed to our first-column goal *and* are able to take responsibility for our own second-column behaviors, then it is likely that the dissonance experienced in working through this column will motivate us to alleviate the tension in some way. If we allow ourselves to learn from our behaviors, we open ourselves to discover rich resources for more fully realizing our true commitment to change.

Column 3 has a "worry box" at the top. Here you will ask yourself, When I consider changing the second-column behaviors to better realize the commitment in column 1, do I feel fear, discomfort, or a sense of loss? As your feelings come to you, allow yourself to stay with them for a while. Then write what you fear or feel uncomfortable about in the worry box. The aim of this column is not to stay with the fears, but to see how you are unconsciously committed to actually protecting yourself from your fears or concerns.

Now move to the bottom half of this third column and ask yourself, what is my commitment to avoiding this fear, discomfort, or sense of loss? What you put in this third column should indicate some commitment to protecting yourself from your fear of concern; that is, to self-preservation. In other words, if your third-column commitment sounds too noble, it is quite likely that you have not touched on your fears or sense of loss. One way to assess if you are taking full advantage of this learning opportunity is to ask about the degree of discomfort you have with your findings. Paradoxically, being very uncomfortable with your responses to these questions is a good sign. The discomfort opens up the possibility for discovering the larger forces that keep you from realizing your first-column commitment.

As figure 9.1 shows, when Michael imagined changing his second-column behaviors, he feared a loss of civility that was very important to him. He also feared a loss of control, should the conflict escalate. What he also worried about was the loss of respect he would have for others, as well as himself, should he actually get involved in conflict. And then as he thought more about what it would be like for him to speak up when he did not agree with the prevailing opinion, he feared that he would lose the positive regard of those who mean a lot to him and support him in his ministry. These worries led him to see that he was also committed to ensuring that he be seen as a person who is nice to everyone and does not take sides or support conflict. Remember what I said about not staying with too noble a competing commitment? If Michael had stayed with his first fear, which he named as his loss of civility, he could have easily indicated that he was also committed to civility. Civility is a noble value and being committed to it is a noble commitment. However, as he thought about his commitment to avoiding that fear, he came to see that for him civility was really about being nice to everyone and maintaining peace at all costs.

Let's now look at the first three columns of Michael's mental map to see how his immune system is keeping him from realizing his first-column commitment. Here we notice that the information in the first and third columns is contradictory. Michael is committed to "developing greater confidence in dealing with conflict," *and* he is committed to "ensuring that he is seen and known as a person who is nice to everyone and does not take sides or support conflict." We can also see that his second-column behaviors are working to ensure that he is known as being nice to everyone. And yet, he is also very committed to dealing with conflict. Kegan and Lahey write, "The problem is not that we are self-protective, but that we are often unaware of being so."[16] By surfacing our competing commitments, we are able to recognize that we have inner contradictions and that they are a valuable source of challenge and growth. In Michael's mental map, the third column reveals the strength of the dynamic force that keeps him from realizing his first-column commitment. The arrows between the first and third columns in the four-column template show that our immune system is made up of counterbalancing motions that actually keep us in a process of dynamic equilibrium.[17]

COLUMN 4: LANGUAGE OF BIG ASSUMPTIONS WE HOLD

The fourth column is designed to reveal our hidden big assumptions that anchor our immune system in place. A big assumption is the ultimate logic *through* which we make meaning of our experience. The language of this column aims to transform our habitual language of "big assumptions we *have*."[18] When big assumptions are hidden from our consciousness, they have us. They have the power to shape how we understand the world and how we act. When we become aware of the "big assumptions we *hold*," we look *at* them rather than *through* them. We can take perspective on them and become responsible for them. We have more of a chance of controlling them, rather than their controlling us. As you will see in the paragraph that follows, naming big assumptions usually takes us into what Kegan and Lahey call "highly consequential territory;" that is, if we do not fulfill our competing commitment, then the consequences can be dire.[19]

To begin working with column 4, look at your third-column entry and ask yourself, if I were *not* committed to what is in column 3, then what would my ministry (or life) be like for me? In using the logic of the "if . . . then" phrase, we begin by negating the competing commitment and then adding the consequences to not fulfilling that commitment. In Michael's case, he begins his fourth-column entry with "*If* I do not ensure that others see me as a person who is nice to everyone and does not take sides or support conflict . . ." He then concludes his sentence with what for him could be the most dire consequence of not realizing his third-column commitment. Here he adds, "*then* I will be seen as a troublemaker and they will lose confidence in me. This could lead to my being rejected as a minister." Without his realizing it, Michael's big assumption had set the terms for his ministry.

As you see in Michael's mental map, the arrow from the fourth into the second column shows how the big assumption grounds and sustains the immune system. The assumption in column 4 is behind the competing commitment in column 3, which in turn generates the behaviors noted in column 2. And as you have already seen, the column 2 behaviors prevent the commitment in column 1 from being fully realized. By identifying big assumptions, we can begin to loosen the hold of unspoken and in some cases unconscious rules that keep us immune to the change to which we are truly committed.

The fourth column closes the initial phase of the immunity-to-change exercise. The follow-up work is represented by the shaded column at the end of the four column exercise. This is an important phase with its own set of requirements that enables us to observe our big assumptions at work, seek out their roots, and test the validity of our assumptions. Without it, the initial phase may be just another opportunity for us to get a glimpse of possibilities for change but then revert to our same behaviors and submerge our new self-awareness.

SHADED COLUMN: FOLLOW-UP WORK

The follow-up phase is a time for becoming even more aware of the ways in which we resist making the change to which we are truly committed. As we observe and test the validity of our big assumption, we can feel threatened and unbalanced. Some of you might feel that your very self is under siege. That is quite normal, and it is for this reason that you are well supported in your follow-up work. It can be done individually with your supervisor-mentor, your theological field educator, or one of your peers. It can also be done in small peer groups or reflective seminars. No matter what the design, you should have an appropriate balance between support and challenge so that you can safely gain perspective on and examine the meanings that no longer fit with your new experiences and understandings.

To show how this phase works, we will continue to follow Michael's developmental path. You can also follow the steps listed in figure 9.2. The first step in this phase is to simply observe your big assumption in action. This means that you do not change your behaviors but simply observe how your big assumption actually affects your actions. After Michael completed his four-column exercise, he was admittedly taken aback. He had not realized the extent to which his own self-image was so deeply intertwined with his big assumption. His first instinct was to just change his behaviors. After all,

FIGURE 9.2: Follow-up Phase

1. Observe your big assumption in action.
2. Be attentive to the experiences that call your big assumption into question.
3. Write the biography of your assumption.
4. Design a first test that will challenge your big assumption.
5. Examine the results of your first test.
6. Develop, run, and evaluate further tests.

when he tried to be rational about his big assumption, he could not understand how he could possibly believe that. However, when he observed his habitual behaviors in avoiding conflict and not speaking up, especially in the congregation to which he was assigned, he certainly acted like the assumption was true, at least most of the time.

The second step is to be attentive to the experiences that call your big assumptions into question. Michael found that he had less difficulty speaking up and addressing conflict within the youth group where he was well regarded by the younger people as well as the adults with whom he shared leadership for that group. He spent some time reflecting on his findings with his supervisor-mentor and with his peers in a weekly seminar. These conversations helped him to see how he was more secure in certain situations, especially those in which his authority was less open to challenge.

The next phases can take you into the messy work of digging up the root of your big assumption. For Michael, the big "aha" came when he reflected on the language rules in his family of origin. At the beginning of the chapter, you were introduced to Michael's experience of growing up in a family where everyone had to speak nicely to each other, even when they felt angry or hurt by another. However, rather than work at saying his truth in a way that respected all, he frequently chose to either avoid conflict or make peace at all costs between his brothers and sisters, especially those who were older than he. He came to see that he had unconsciously internalized those language rules as part of his own identity, seeing himself as a nice, peaceful person. They not only regulated how he acted but also shaped is own self-image. In making his new awareness explicit in conversations with his supervisor-mentor as well as his peers, he began to see how much power he had given to his big assumption; yet, he also realized it did not have to determine his destiny. As he looked *at* his assumption and began to question it, he gradually saw that dealing with conflict did not always mean being aggressive or confrontational. We do not come to that awareness simply through a technical fix of developing skills for dealing with conflict. Unless Michael had explored the root of his big assumption that kept his immune system in balance, he was doomed to not realizing the commitment to which he was truly committed.

The next step is to design a test that will challenge your big assumptions. With the support of his supervisor-mentor, Michael planned that he would intentionally stay present (not withdraw) if the conflict arose at the next altar guild meeting. Sure enough, it did, and not only did he stay present but he also built up the courage to share with the group what he saw as the key issue in the conflict. While some members of the guild were taken aback with his forwardness, others thought that his intervention helped the group become more honest about its ongoing conflict. A subsequent debriefing with his supervisor-mentor and peers allowed him to make further tests of his assumption in the altar guild meetings until he became more and more confident in his dealing with conflict. Although Michael is continuing to work to even more fully realize this goal, openly engaging in conflictual situations has become more natural for him than it was before.

When planning your own follow-up phase, keep in mind that like the four-column exercise, the follow-up phase is designed as a sequence of steps aimed at gradually and safely disturbing the inner logic of the big assumption. Do not try to rush and fix the problem too quickly. Like New Year's resolutions, that approach offers only short-term remedies and superficial change. Allow the follow-up phase to be a space for a deeper and long-lasting change. This will enable you to become more authentic in your leadership. And when you find that you have successfully achieved your goal, you can repeat this exercise with other commitments that are important to developing your leadership potential.

For Supervisor-Mentors

In this part of the chapter, we will again draw upon the wisdom of Kegan and Lahey who offer two other practical languages to transform our more habitual forms of social communication in order to provide optimal support for students' growth.

THE LANGUAGE OF ONGOING REGARD

We all know the importance of being affirmed in what we do. Without affirmation, it is difficult for anyone to stay open to learning. The way we usually express our valuing of another person's behavior or intention is by using the language of ongoing regard.[20] We can express our ongoing regard in two different ways—appreciation and admiration—each of which has a different orientation and effect. Many of us habitually communicate our ongoing regard by expressing admiration for the person. For example, when Michael's supervisor-mentor observed Michael testing his big assumption by voicing his opinion in the altar guild meeting, he could have expressed admiration by saying, "Michael, you are very courageous." In giving this kind of feedback, the supervisor-mentor is bestowing on Michael his own interpretation of Michael's worthiness. It would have been a judgment on Michael's value or quality as a person. In contrast, if he had communicated his ongoing regard by expressing appreciation for Michael, he might have said, "I really appreciate how you led that meeting last evening, Michael. Your way of surfacing and reframing some of the underlying currents helped the group to begin taking ownership of some of its own unaddressed issues." Useful and supportive feedback expressed as appreciation is concrete and gives specific information about the student's behavior itself as well as its impact on you or others. Furthermore, when you offer appreciation in a timely manner, it has even greater potential for making a difference in the student's learning.

LANGUAGE OF DECONSTRUCTIVE CRITICISM

When we consider giving feedback to someone, we will most often make the distinction between giving constructive or destructive criticism. We have all been exposed to both, and most likely been trained to deliver criticism of the constructive kind that aims to be positive and build up the person. And while few would argue that this is the right kind of feedback to offer your students, a number of assumptions lie behind constructive criticism. For example, when we offer critical feedback, even of the constructive type, we assume we have the right interpretation of the situation and most likely the right answers. The feedback is usually offered because we want the other to change.

Kegan and Lahey offer another alternative form of feedback that they call the "language of deconstructive criticism" that is consistent with the insights of the four column exercise.[21] Just as the language suggests, when we deconstruct something, we take it apart, usually to see why it is not working. That is what this language is designed to do: take apart or loosen up our certitudes in order to gain a more expansive understanding of the problem at hand. Rather than simply focusing on trying to get others to change their behaviors, it creates a context for exploring the meanings and assumptions that both parties bring to the situation.[22] Practicing this language does not mean we give up our own view; however, we hold it a little more tentatively, risking the input of others to question or even change it. In some cases, our own perspectives may make a lot of sense to other people; however, when we try to understand their own perspectives, we may come to see how difficult it is for them to give up or change their own meanings.[23]

For example, Michael's supervisor-mentor chose to look at his own assumptions about Michael and his way of dealing with conflict. His own understanding of our built-in immunity to change gave him the language and tools to explore with Michael ways he could achieve his most important learning goal. This kind of conversation was most helpful for Michael's learning throughout the follow-up phase, particularly when he designed and tested his big assumption in the altar guild.

Throughout this chapter, I have claimed that language creates our reality. I believe that in practicing the languages in this chapter, we can fashion language communities in which students can, as David Day calls for, become "prepared to participate in the process of leadership as the situation demands and as challenging events unfold."[24] Our congregations deserve that quality of leadership.

Language and Leadership

FIGURE 9.3: Four Column Exercise Worksheet
copyright © Minds at Work

1 LANGUAGE OF COMMITMENT	2 LANGUAGE OF PERSONAL RESPONSIBILITY	3 LANGUAGE OF COMPETING COMMITMENTS	4 LANGUAGE OF ASSUMPTIONS WE HOLD
I am committed to ...	What am I doing or not doing?	I am also committed to...	If I ..., then ...
		Worry Box	

10
Considerations for Cross-Cultural Placement

JOANNE LINDSTROM

Field education—the "Final Frontier" . . . Well, not exactly! For some students, field studies or supervised ministry or ministry in context, however named, can seem as though it is such. There is a sense of traveling to a galaxy far, far away—entry into an unfamiliar culture with unknown language, customs, food, attire, art, history, sacred expressions, perhaps even an unknown God. What an adventure!

There are a multitude of lenses through which to view an unfamiliar culture. The four most commonly named are race, gender, ethnicity, and language. Students often enter a new context focusing primarily on The Other—often discounting the particularities and cultural formations of their own lives. Students come to field education shaped by countless cultural components and innumerable experiences, both tiny and huge. If you are entering a new field education setting, your ability to articulate your own uniqueness and particularities will help you appreciate, minister to, and understand those with whom you serve, as you seek to honor universal human experiences mediated by your own individual distinctiveness, including race, gender, ethnicity, and language.

We are inclined to consider race, gender, ethnicity, and language as the only important elements in our own formation, but countless other components contribute to individual uniqueness and vision of the world. Age, skin color, physical ability, height, weight, education, marital status, nationality, adoption, military experience, economic status, geographic location, religion, birth order, sexual orientation, worship experiences, extended family, political persuasion—all of these are relevant, and the list goes on.

Given such an open-ended list of factors that form us, how, then, do we live and minister with one another, honoring our own God-given creatureliness as we meet others in a new and unfamiliar setting? How do we grow into competent leaders able to minister with agility and humility across the diverse cultures and contexts in which we find ourselves? What capacities do we need to develop and what attributes do we need to nurture for ministry and leadership in the church and world?

Sacred texts offer wisdom and guidance for the challenging questions of cross-cultural engagement. One helpful framework is found in Rom. 12:1–3:

> I appeal to you therefore, brothers and sisters, by the mercies of God, to present your bodies as a living sacrifice, holy and acceptable to God, which is your spiritual worship. Do not be conformed to this world, but be transformed by the renewing of your minds, so that you may discern what is the will of God—what is good and acceptable and perfect. For by the grace given to me I say to everyone among you not to think of yourself more highly than you ought to think, but to think with sober judgment, each according to the measure of faith that God has assigned.

Themes from this text can assist us in engaging in a new cultural context: nonconformity, transformation, and sober judgment.

Do Not Be Conformed

"Do not be conformed to this world," Paul writes. Do not sustain and maintain the customary patterns and behaviors of the world that demean human beings. Whether customary patterns and behaviors explicitly reinforce ways people are demeaned according to race, gender, language, or ethnicity, or whether these patterns and behaviors operate more subtly, devaluing others based on marital status, physical ability, or education, and so on, we are continually called to challenge ourselves to look, love, and live beyond incomplete descriptions of The Other. This challenge does not call us to ignore cultural differences but to live in community with the tension of various personal distinctions.

The nonconformity of which the apostle Paul speaks is an expression of God's grace in the structuring of human relationships. Restructuring of human relationships can be tricky as we enter new cultural contexts. In general, our tendency is to interact with others based on one of two polarities. We may be tempted to use our own experiences and understandings as the criteria to which others should conform, viewing the new context through our own lenses without questions or critical reflection, assuming our experience is normative, perhaps even God-ordained. Or we may be tempted to conform to the norms of the new cultural context, dismissing without questions or critical reflection the validity of our own experiences, viewing a new cultural context as normative—superior to our own and, yes, perhaps even God-ordained.

The supervisor-mentor is an important resource in navigating this unknown territory. She or he models appropriate ministry for the context and assists in examining the similarities and differences between your own context and the unfamiliar environment. Together, supervisor-mentor and intern explore implications for the practice of ministry and operating from one context or the other—or from a courageous and creative intersection of these two contexts.

Be Transformed

The continuing transformation of the people of God requires far more than a tweaking of externals—wearing Afrocentric clothing in February to celebrate Black History Month or putting on a clerical collar. Transformation is complete change—metamorphosis.

It is authentically appropriating new ideas and attitudes that give the experience of self and others greater depth and sophistication. Transformation moves us beyond how we once understood and experienced ourselves into a "new creation" (2 Cor. 5:17).

Transformation doesn't just fall on us like manna from heaven. As biblical scholar Thomas L. Hoyt Jr. reminds us, "This transformation is not a one-time event but a constant struggle."[1] It is based on commitment to the renewing of one's mind, requiring engagement with consistent, critical theological reflection. Such reflection pays careful attention to ways that biblical texts relate to the rituals and practices of a faith community. It urges full engagement with supervisors and lay teams, listening to their experiences, sharing our own, humbly questioning both as we allow God to speak through Scripture, tradition, and experience. It requires courage to look deeply into oneself and one's own cultural context and assumptions as we offer our lives to be shaped by grace rather than the world.

Exercise Sober Judgment

As field studies students and future ministerial leaders, exploring our self-understanding in our particular context is critical. Paul urges us not to think too highly of ourselves (and I would add, too lowly) but to think about ourselves with sober judgment. Sober judgment is thoughtful and discerning. Acquiring such judgment often involves significant sacrifice. This kind of knowing requires rugged honesty with oneself and with others. It raises the question of how honest I want to be with myself,[2] and how honest I dare to be with others. Addressing these questions is not for the faint of heart.

Eric Law, Episcopal priest, author, and founding director of Kaleidoscope Institute, defines self-awareness as a "deep understanding of one's cultural values, strengths and weaknesses, and privileges and power that come with one's roles and cultural background."[3] Self-awareness is more than simply identifying the various cultural components that make up identity. Sober judgment is questioning, exploring, digging deep to understand how those components influence our way of experiencing the world. As we continue the journey into self-awareness, honoring the complexity of our own lives, we become better able to honor the complexities of another's life, appreciating differences as opportunities, rather than problems.[4] As we are better able to articulate our own strengths and weakness, we can more fully accept the strengths and weaknesses of others.

Reflecting on Cross-Cultural Relationships

In the broader U.S. culture, race, gender, ethnicity, and language are often perceived as the only obstacles or challenges to cross-cultural relationships. However, as the following brief study will show, cross-cultural relationships can be hindered by more subtle cultural components.

Two students, Andrew and Amy, were both placed at the same church for their year of supervised ministry. This church was located in a neighborhood different from where either one of them had worshiped or served. Both students had earned master's degrees in other helping professions and were employed in positions of responsibility prior to entering the Master of Divinity program. The two students had a common denominational affiliation and had served in various capacities in their home congregations. Both home congregations were grounded in a black church tradition valuing vibrant, enthusiastic, call-and-response worship, complete with gospel choirs and artful oratory. Leadership was strongly focused on the pastor.

A contextual nuance peculiar to Chicago reflects migration patterns of African Americans within the city and differences between Southsiders and Westsiders. Both students were Westsiders; the field site congregation was South Side. Colloquially speaking, Southsiders refer to Westsiders as "ghetto," as a way of delineating differing strata of class, education, and economic status.

The church where Andrew and Amy were placed for their year of field studies also belonged to the same denomination as their home congregation. However, the field site was quite different from what either had experienced previously. The worship music of this church tended to be classical, using hymns and anthems rather than gospel music or choruses. The worship setting was much quieter, with less call and response. Lay leaders participated in worship to a greater degree than either student had previously experienced. The pastor preached from the Revised Common Lectionary, and the worship services reflected the seasons of the liturgical year.

As part of their field studies program, Amy and Andrew were asked to reflect on what challenged them and what helped them flourish in their new context. Both Andrew and Amy were challenged by the very different style of worship. Having come from a worship style where "I got to get my praise on!" with emotive physicality of worship being the evidence of God's presence, worship at the field site initially left them cold, confused, and questioning.

OBSERVING AND ABSORBING

Andrew's response to the unfamiliar worship experiences led him to join the male chorus at the field site congregation. For the first time, he used sheet music, and for the first time in years he used a hymnal. In a reflection time with the field educator, he spoke about Psa. 137:4: "How could we sing the LORD's song in a foreign land?" For him, singing the Lord's song in a strange land wasn't geographical but rather theological and experiential.

In time, Andrew recognized that his struggles originated not so much from the field site as from inside himself. "I rushed into judgment before I observed or absorbed" the genuine worship at the field site, he said. He assumed that quieter worship services only happened in white churches and struggled to see how worshipers at his field site were as involved as worshipers in his home church. Andrew named his stereotyping behavior and judgment as coming from his own fear—fear of leaving the congregation where he was raised; fear about whether his gifts and talents would be received; fear of being the outsider and wondering how to fit in to the unfamiliar context.

Another dissimilarity for Andrew was the way titles were understood. After fifteen years of ministry in another congregation where he was called "Reverend" even though he was not ordained, Andrew found himself being called "Minister Andrew" in a congregation that understood titles and ordination differently. At first, to be called "minister" instead of "reverend" felt like a demotion. But as Andrew persevered in his new context, he began to understand and accept the different understanding of titles.

Even in the midst of these difference and challenges, Andrew was thriving. He credited his ability to flourish in this ministry setting, first, to his relationship with his supervisor-mentor, and second, to his relationship with the congregation and their support of not only his ministry but also his wife and children.

In the supervisory relationship, Andrew found a safe place to question his occasional biased experience. "I expect this kind of worship in a white church, not a black church." His supervisor responded openly and without defensiveness, sharing his own life and ministry; the reasons for use of the Revised Common Lectionary and observations of the liturgical calendar.

Andrew identified his relationship with his supervisor-mentor as a primary instrument of his flourishing and learning. In the hospitality of those reflection times, he was able to find a place to "block out differences and listen to the similarities." He began to be intentional about embracing changes that he experienced in worship and to see that "the people were into what they were doing—genuine worship." Andrew was even able to see that the congregation included some folks who "worship like me." He was able to name and honor both experiences, observing, "I like to say I come from a traditional black Baptist church but this church is traditional, too!"

The congregation's care was the other component in Andrew's flourishing. Members invested in Andrew's learning and development and in his wife, Jenna, and their children. Perhaps their most influential, generous act of caring had to do with Andrew's spouse. Jenna had responded to God's call to ordained ministry and entered seminary, but in Andrew's home congregation, women in ministry were not supported, and he knew it was only a matter of time until he would have to leave his home congregation for good. This field site congregation embraced Jenna's call and took her under their care—the first woman this congregation has formally supported in the journey toward ordained ministry.

In other reflections, Andrew offered the following advice to students entering the field studies experience, especially those who find themselves in sites that they expect to be familiar:

> Learn to live with ambiguities and questions.
> Know that God is big—*huge*.
> Be grateful for the opportunity to encounter God.
> Put yourself out—don't resist change.
> Be willing to learn the deeper culture, hidden beyond what is seen and heard.

REEVALUATING IDENTITY

Amy, as Andrew, also experienced the challenge of a "more mainstream worship style" at the field site congregation. This was heightened due to how she apprehended "the church's perception" of class and educational differences and people "coming from the right family." As the first one in her working class family to graduate from college, successfully complete one master's degree, and now pursue a second, Amy initially had difficulty navigating what she perceived as elitism. She struggled with a sense that the worship style of the field site was better than that of her home congregation. This was directly connected to her fear of leaving her home congregation because of both the comfort she found in the worship experience's familiarity and the fact that she shared it with her family. Amy's education and professional accomplishments had already set her apart from others in her family system, and this would be yet another experience that would emphasize the increasing differences.

The challenges Amy experienced were rooted in her sense of identity as one shaped and formed by what she understood as the "traditional" black church. This experience called her to reevaluate her identity, her role in her family, and God's purpose for her life. In the midst of these challenges, Amy named the congregation as an important factor in her flourishing. Through her relationships with members of the congregation, she began to see evidence of her own growth, changes, even transformations. Through the struggle of comparing the field site worship style with her preferred and familiar style, she was able to see a "lot of paradigm shifts," not the least of which was the realization that "God can be in more than one context" and that she was "able to see God" in both.

As members of the congregation shared their lives, stories, and life journeys, Amy perceived commonalities among the different expressions of worship. Music was often the "same music but sung differently" and served the same function—a way to praise and honor God. Some use anthems, others use gospel. Liturgical dance could be "ballet-ish and modern with a little hip-hop thrown in." Amy was able to experience the worship service as having the same purpose but a different expression than what she was accustomed to. The preaching was similar, "less the call and response" but theologically deep and nurturing for the congregation. She, like Andrew, was able to see some "folks who worship like me." Amy was grateful for what she called the "privilege" and gift of this learning experience: "I have known myself to be a change agent, and this opportunity has been to be on the other end with God being the change agent!"

MENTORING THAT CHALLENGES AND ENCOURAGES

Amy and Andrew were under the care of a seasoned supervisor who was able to facilitate growth and transformation. As he reflected on his experience with each student, he named consistent supervisory sessions as indispensable components of the learning and growing process. As supervisor, he was clear about his own style (direct) and aware of how each of the students had their own styles of reflection and their own responses to his style. The supervisor was clear that his role had multiple components. He was called to facilitate growth and transformation by challenging their reflection, by providing opportunities for their learning and serving, and by sharing his own faith and pastoral journey. In addition, he encouraged the congregation to share their individual and collective faith journeys. This helped the students understand the context in which they found themselves, even as they found their own authentic voice. This required attention to each student's distinctive styles and learning goals, their ability to observe and understand a context, and their experiences and exposure to varieties of intercultural experiences both within the African American community and beyond. His challenge was to discern how far to push when encountering resistance or "when there is a block."

The supervisor responded to the students' struggle with worship style by continuing to push them to be both observant of and open to the possibility of new ways to experience God that would allow for varieties of expression rather than just "one diet." He encouraged them to move into this different cultural context and challenged their cultural assumptions regarding "the black church." Both Andrew and Amy expressed appreciation that they were able to learn about their own culture and acknowledge that there is no monolithic black church but rather a broad, deep, diverse African American Christian experience.

This study illustrates how students can move away from the either-or understanding of normative experiences and embrace transformation as they continue to develop their own sober, sound judgment. Both Andrew and Amy entered the field studies experience certain that their preferred worship style was the one true worship style. How could one tell if the Spirit was present if there were no verbal responses and exultations during the worship service? At the outset, they used their own experience as the criterion for what is normative.

Through reflection with their supervisor and the larger congregation, they were able to integrate new ideas and attitudes that allowed them to perceive and appreciate diversity. Amy and Andrew engaged in consistent ministerial reflection with their supervisor and members of the congregation, and through encounters with this congregation's understanding of God, tradition, worship, Scriptures, and leadership, they were able to hear God speaking differently. Scholar Thomas L. Hoyt Jr. says, "Paul calls for the transformation of the mind, because he knows that actions are generated by attitudes."[5] Andrew and Amy's actions and acceptance of experiencing God in new ways illustrate such transformation through the renewing of the mind.

Inner Transformation

Another way to view this transformation process is through the insights of Carl G. Jung, who writes, "The patient must be drawn out 'of himself' into other paths, which is the true meaning of 'education,' and this can only be achieved by an educative will."[6] While field studies students are not patients, transformation does require that they are willing to be drawn out of themselves and into the paths of others, all the while being willing to be changed by God's Spirit through those encounters.

Pastoral theologian Jaco Hamman writes that "knowledge rarely leads to change" and encourages us to engage relationships and experiences with compassionate curiosity and questions about ourselves.[7] He calls us to develop capacities—a roominess that can hold the questions, the tensions, and the paradoxes that we have within us. Both Amy and Andrew, through the process of reflection and questioning, were able to create and develop a larger inner self that could hold their own sense of self, which in turn makes available greater capacities to honor others. Without their judgmental lens, both Andrew and Amy entered relationships, worship experiences, and responsibilities with greater grace and love and with more agility and freedom.

The development and acceptance of our self, our gifts and graces for ministry as well as our limitations, are critical for ministry and for exploring and celebrating one's particular place in ministry. This requires courage to engage in ongoing self-assessment and evaluation and to develop relationships with peers and colleagues who will hold us accountable to ongoing self-reflection about our cultural particularities and how we affect and interact with others.

The experiences of Andrew and Amy can be a helpful guide to ongoing development and pastoral formation as it relates to ministry across diverse contexts. While actual, tangible ministry skills are necessary—listening skills, preaching, teaching, administration, worship leadership, pastoral care, and so on—a requisite would be more about attitude than aptitude, more soul-based than skill-based, more about courage than capability. For Andrew and Amy to grow, they had to engage questions about their own faith journey and the faith journeys of others. They had to develop and nurture attitudes of compassionate curiosity about themselves and the context in which they were serving and learning.

To move into the transformation stage, Amy and Andrew had to participate in new experiences. They had to evoke courage and a willingness to learn and grow; to entertain new understandings of God and God's activity in the world. They had to offer their own bodies, minds, and souls to God as their spiritual worship, relying on God to renew their minds.

Amy and Andrew were then able to articulate their own growth—recognizing the narrowness of their experience and how their lack of exposure to wider community understandings limited their abilities. They were able to identify areas of ongoing growth as they both desired to have the necessary agility and humility to minister in whatever context God offers.

The first practical component providing such a nurturing environment was the supervisor. In this particular case, the supervisor was able to hear critique and criticism without responding defensively. He held differing viewpoints and experiences without humiliating the students. He attended respectfully to each, sensitive to their individual learning styles, yet appropriately challenged their perceptions and judgments. The supervisor was able to do this largely because he took the time to develop trust with the students early in the placement process. As a result, he was able to push and challenge; and the students knew that he had their best interests, growth, and ministry in mind.

The second critical component was the hospitality of the congregation. They understood themselves as a teaching congregation and also had the ability to hold differing experiences without defensiveness. They very clearly wanted the students to succeed, grow, and develop as mature disciples of Christ and ministers of the gospel. The congregation had an appropriate pride in the students' accomplishments and expressed gratitude for being part of the journey.

Because supervised ministry programs are so diverse, a classroom component may or may not be connected to the experiential component. However, a peer group or ministry reflection group is often required. This is another important element of growth and development. It provides an opportunity to develop colleague relationships that will assist students in self-assessment and evaluation, and offer wisdom and questions for discernment.

The journey of cross-cultural placement requires great effort, intent, and compassion. However, as students continue to grow in self-understanding, dare to be honest about their own cultural makeup, and courageously share themselves and the lives of others with respect and care, the foundation for rewarding ministry is created.

11

Assessment and Theological Field Education

SARAH B. DRUMMOND

The words *assessment* and *evaluation* can elevate the heart rates of the full range of partners in theological field education: supervisors, students, and congregations. Students who have contemplated a sense of call to ministry might view field education as an audition, a test of their abilities. They think the evaluations they experience throughout seminary could either prove that they were right in pursuing their calling or raise serious questions about whether ministry is right for them.

Supervisor-mentors sometimes view their effectiveness in working with students as a test of their own competence, and they believe that their reputation in the field might be influenced by how students rate and describe the coaching they receive. Congregations make themselves vulnerable when they open their doors and hearts to students, and around evaluation time leaders worry about how feedback might be received by students and what feedback they might get in return. Especially in cases where tensions and conflicts have arisen in the field education year, formal assessment processes provoke anxiety about the future effects the documents such processes produce might have on all participants in student learning.

Although this anxiety is real, its roots dig into fundamental misunderstandings about the meaning and purpose of assessment in theological field education. Student experiential learning is not primarily an exercise in determining fitness for ministry, although it provides helpful evidence for those engaged in that determination. Field education is not designed to give the supervisor-mentor a chance to shine, although some ministers do discover a special gift for the work of supporting student learning. Congregations' lives are often enriched by the ministry of those newer to the field and excited about the future, but they also take a risk when they provide balanced—rather than one-sidedly positive—feedback to student ministers. Related to all of these underlying misconceptions is the one this chapter seeks most ardently to upset: the belief that assessment is about passing judgment.

Assessment in theological field education is not the verdict that comes at the end of students' service, but rather it is part of the learning process from beginning to end. *In field education, assessment, and the formal evaluation practices that assessments include, is the accountability process that accompanies and deepens student learning.* The field-education-student learning-assessment process takes place in four phases:

Phase 1: The student frames learning goals in collaboration with supervisor-mentors, teachers who have insights into the student's vocational aspirations, and congregations that provide opportunities to minister and reflect.

Phase 2: The student creates an action plan for meeting these goals.

Phase 3: The student implements the action plan, under supervision and through theological reflection practices.

Phase 4: At certain intervals, usually once midyear and once after service is complete, the partners in the student's learning revisit these goals, address successes and gaps, and write formal evaluations both midcourse (formative evaluations) and at the end of service (summative evaluations).

Whereas evaluation practices, such as midyear progress reports and final evaluations, are part of assessment, assessment is much more than measuring hopes against results at particular moments in the year. Instead, assessment is the means through which the work of field education becomes not just a set of tasks but a means for growth for an adult learner who is capable of implementing an ambitious learning plan under supervision.

For the Student

Julia, an M.Div. student, sees an e-mail in her inbox with an attachment from her supervisor-mentor in her field education site. She knows it is the draft of his section of her midyear progress report. She drags her cursor over it and hesitates, thinking, What might Bruce have said about me? In their most recent weekly meeting, Bruce raised some concerns he had about her public presence in worship. Her voice sounded small, he said, and her insistence on using a manuscript put a barrier between her and the congregation.

Julia is, in fact, a relatively petite person with a naturally high-pitched voice. In the past, when she had tried to project her voice from the pulpit, she had gotten the feedback that her voice sounded painfully shrill. And honestly, she does not trust her memory enough to rise to the pulpit without notes, as the paper in front of her gives her courage that she will not just ramble on when offering something as important as a pastoral prayer. Leading others in prayer feels like such a big responsibility, making the possibility of squeaking or babbling when leading horrifying. When Julia tried to share this with Bruce, he raised questions about her ability to hear feedback. Now she is relatively sure he will have written negative comments into his midyear evaluation and probably will never recommend her for ordination or a future ministry job. At least that is what Julia is thinking as her cursor hovers on the screen.

Most adults have had an experience like Julia's, worrying about how their superior will evaluate them. With such worries come not just embarrassment but also fear about the long-term career implications of written evaluative documents and verbal judgments. To a certain extent, assessment in field education provokes anxiety in that it raises questions about fitness for ministry and a student's ability to learn and grow. Formal evaluation processes place students in a vulnerable position, and subjectivity and human foibles add further uncertainty to that vulnerability.

Perhaps the best antidote for this anxiety is to understand the way in which formal evaluation processes fit into an overarching student learning assessment process, and to make sure that all partners in student learning share this understanding. By seeing assessment as an accountability infrastructure meant to support student growth and learning, all parties see evaluation as just one part of the picture, and assessment more as a tool for learning than as a gauge for measuring fitness.

Students are at the center of the process, driving it forward rather than allowing it to happen to them. They must remember that assessment is not about other people passing judgment on them. Through assessment, students hold themselves accountable to the learning process, which not only deepens their learning but also teaches them skills for lifelong growth and improvement in their practice of ministry. On page 170 I wrote about four phases of assessment in field education. Here I will describe the role of the *student* in each of these phases.

PHASE 1

The student collaboratively frames learning goals.

Students should begin to establish their learning goals before they even begin field education. Depending on where contextual or field education is located in the student's degree program sequence, students have more or less time in seminary to consider what they most want to learn. Those who have a full year of seminary before field education have the benefit of numerous conversations with peers and professors about their strengths and growth areas, hopes for the future, and gaps in their knowledge.

Whether students begin field education right away or well into a degree program, they should never try to frame goals alone. Students' perspective on what they need to learn in order to enter ministry will be limited in part by their lack of experience; even those who come to seminary after many years of high-level lay leadership will not have perfect insight into what ministers need to be able to do. Similarly, students' perspective on their learning needs will be limited the way it is for all people: We only can know partly our own strengths and weaknesses, and we rely on others to help us see ourselves more clearly.

Some good questions for a student to bring to professors, peers, pastors, denominational leaders, and even family members include the following:

- What am I already good at, to the point that I do not need to spend a lot of time on it in field education?
- Where are the biggest gaps in my abilities?
- I do not know what I do not know: What blind spots about my own ministerial effectiveness and the nature of ministry can another point out to me?

Field education is a time for experimentation, so students should consider a wide range of ministry areas about which to learn through tasks and reflection. Students in field education often find themselves in the position where they must dive into a ministry task without any previous experience. Therefore, when setting goals, the student should expect to feel that some are risky, taking them into new territory, without any idea of whether they will be good at the task ahead of time. Experienced supervisor-mentors and congregational leaders understand that students are often trying on tasks, and even the ministerial identity, for the first time. Though some might argue that repetition is not the only way a person learns a skill, no one would argue that a person could master a skill the first time one performs it. And that first time has to come sometime; when better than field education?

Once students have come to some level of understanding about their strengths and growth areas heading into field education, they must work with supervisor-mentors and congregational leaders to learn about the ministry opportunities available to them in the site.

Imagine a student, for example, who has no experience working with youth who hears from his learning support network that this is a liability he must address. If his field education congregation has only a handful of youth, and the lay leader who works with those youth might not feel comfortable with a student minister as a short-term coleader, this learning gap might not be addressed through field education. Depending on how the student's seminary arranges field education placements, perhaps this site would not be right for the student. Or perhaps he will meet this learning goal through another part of his education; field education cannot, after all, give a student every learning opportunity she or he needs.

Students are often tempted, when framing goals, to be abstract and lofty. Although there is room for philosophical and even grandiose goal setting in field education, balance with the practical is important as well. In many field education programs, students write a learning covenant that they submit about six weeks into their field education year. At Andover Newton Theological School, we have a document that guides this process. It encourages students to create goal statements that are big and bold: "I want to learn what it means to be a parish minister with a commitment to social justice." "I want to learn to be an effective leader for a church-related educational institution." "I want to learn to provide a nonanxious and compassionate presence to the dying and their families." None of these goals could be met in one year, and one might argue that even a lifetime of service would not be enough time to learn all of the intricacies of these goals, but we encourage students to orient themselves through this goal setting toward a general direction that will guide their next steps.

PHASE 2

The student creates an action plan for meeting these goals.

After setting a goal, the student then gets specific about the objectives that will, together, help the student meet the goal. For example, let us consider the goal, "I want to learn what it means to be a parish minister with a commitment to social justice." What might be some related objectives?

- To learn to lead public worship on Sundays in such a way that participants are empowered and encouraged to minister to the world throughout the week.
- To learn to coordinate partnerships between the church and agencies that serve justice-oriented causes in the community.
- To learn to work collaboratively with lay leaders to plan, serve, and reflect on mission projects in the church.

With each objective, the student then names a series of tasks required to carry out the objectives. At this phase of the learning goal-setting process, collaboration becomes even more crucial. The supervisor-mentor and leaders in the congregation can give the students information about how he or she can get involved in tasks, and they also can help the student gain access to essential opportunities. For instance, consider the first objective: "To learn to lead public worship on Sundays in such a way that participants are empowered and encouraged to minister to the world throughout the week." To achieve this objective, the student must actually participate in planning and leading worship. She or he must preach and pray, call for the offering and thank God for the congregation's generosity, invoke and bless, and do so regularly enough so as to have a baseline of experience upon which to reflect and ideally improve. The learning plan should include as many measurable specifics as possible, including how often the student will lead worship and preach, how much time preparation will take each week, and where such preparation will take place. Why is this necessary? Does ministry not tend to wax and wane and vary week to week? Of course it does. But students are beginners who do not necessarily know from the outset what time and attention ministry tasks will require. Specific intentions will give them a chance to share their assumptions with others with more experience, and written plans will give them a document they can adjust over time as they become more used to the ministry work flow.

Considering that field education students are generally engaging in tasks that are new to them, an important final step in framing learning goals is naming the resources that the students will call upon as they perform tasks. Even though they might be trying new things and stretching into unfamiliar ministry areas, students should not feel that they must do so blindfolded. Therefore, intentionally naming how the student will get the information, counsel, and examples they need before they begin helps all partners in student learning to feel confident that the learner can still serve while learning.

The tasks associated with leading worship are numerous and sometimes nerve-wracking. Therefore, the student should consider in advance what resources will be available to support the work and learning:

- A worship or preaching class at the seminary
- An intentional, weekly prechurch review of the worship order with an experienced worship leader on the congregation's staff
- Sample prayers from the supervisor-mentor

Just because a student is inexperienced does not mean she or he must make forays without adequate preparation. By naming resources, the student finds encouragement while also making a promise to take advantage of the supports available to enable functioning at a high level of professional competence. This process is illustrated in figure 11.1.

Goal setting is the first step in the learning assessment process. By setting learning goals, the student establishes, in collaboration with the supervisor-mentor and congregation, the benchmarks against which his or her progress will be evaluated. Some field education programs provide more structure around student learning goals. For others the goal setting is free-form and up to the student. In either case, assessment without goals against which to assess is simply impossible. Therefore, the quality and integrity of this first

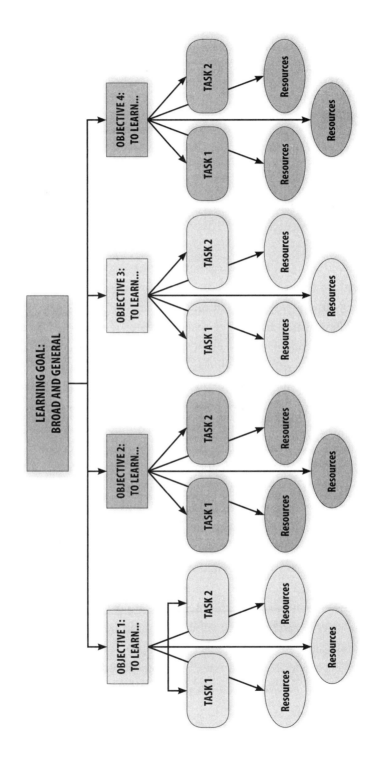

FIGURE 11.1: Learning Goals and Objectives

step of the process is essential to student learning and the overall assessment of it.

PHASE 3

The student implements the action plan, under supervision and through theological reflection practices.

Many field education programs call upon students and supervisor-mentors to meet weekly or biweekly for theological reflection. In those meetings, students talk about the implementation of their learning strategy. They reflect theologically on what they experience, considering ministry events in light of their faith, paying special attention to moments when they discover a disconnect between what they do and what they think they believe.

Few think about a regular practice of theological reflection as part of student learning assessment, but this practice plays a critical role in assessment. As the student lives out learning goals and objectives, he or she performs tasks that provide meaningful data about the student's growth or lack thereof.

At Andover Newton, we require that students write a weekly theological reflection to share with their supervisor before the weekly theological reflection meeting. They write reflections in a two-column format, with their description of a ministry event and initial thoughts on the left and room for supervisor comments on the right. We encourage students to save all of their reflections, printed out and in one place, and to review both those reflections and their learning covenants before engaging in formal evaluation processes. The ministry events students describe provide data or evidence of ministry performed. The reflection students offer about the event, and on which supervisors comment, provides insight into the progress students make as they more deeply understand ministry. As students review their theological reflections written over the course of the year, themes emerge that point to areas where they have learned and grown. Feedback from the supervisor over time can also point to areas where the student has paid attention and might dedicate more energy.

PHASE 4

At certain intervals, the partners in the student's learning revisit these goals, address successes and gaps, and write formal evaluations both midcourse (formative evaluations) and at the end of service (final evaluations).

Ideally, if the student has attended to the previous three steps with care, evaluations take the form of synthesizing their goals, actions, and reflections; seeing the year as a whole with beginning, middle, and end; and chronicling the daily work and major milestones that constitute a year in field education. Such capturing of information is the purpose of formal evaluations, not presenting new information.

At some midpoint in field education, students and their supervisor-mentors, as well as appropriate leaders in the congregation, should review the learning covenant and discuss its implementation so far. Have milestones been reached? Then celebrate. Have certain objectives fallen by the wayside? Then ask why and whether a modification of the covenant is in order. This formative evaluation is an opportunity to think creatively. For example, if a student included among her learning objectives that she wanted to preside over a funeral, but no one in the congregation has (thankfully) died, perhaps she and the supervisor-mentor might reach out to some local funeral homes to inquire about opportunities for her to officiate in or assist with a funeral for a family with no church ties. By coming up for air at the midpoint in field education, course corrections can take place early to prevent the student from ultimately landing at an unintended destination.

In final, or summative, evaluations, the tone is different. Midcourse corrections are no longer possible, and the benefit of hindsight begins to emerge. Final evaluations often take on a more subjective tone, with overall impressions shared about the arc of the student's year. In these evaluations, three practices are crucial for the integrity of the assessment process:

- Honesty. Those writing about the student must be honest about his or her strengths and growth areas, with a strong emphasis on the student's learning rather than performance. At times, supervisor-mentors might prefer to avoid writing about difficult issues that came up during the year—field education is over, after all—but failing to give a full and honest picture does not further student learning.
- Transparency. Evaluation documents are part of the student's educational record and therefore can only be shared with the student's explicit permission. All partners—the student, the supervisor-mentor, and the appropriate leaders in the congregation—should have the opportunity to see each other's writing about the student, and the student should not have to suffer the awkwardness of feeling she or he is being evaluated secretly. I give the strong advice to all partners to discuss any concerns that might appear in evaluations verbally before putting them in writing, as written words are harder to "hear." Transparency, even when sharing hard but honest feedback, is a far healthier form of communication.
- Mutuality. Students do not serve in field education in a vacuum. Much of their learning experience is bound to be shaped by their ministry context and relationship with the supervisor-mentor. Therefore, the student should play an active role in self-assessment as well as evaluating the ministry setting as a learning environment.

So, what if field education just does not go very well? What if goals are not met, if tensions arise in the ministry setting, or if the student and the supervisor-mentor simply do not work well together? The hope is that, through engaging assessment with care and intentionality, students learn a great deal about ministry and about themselves that transcends the actual context where they serve in field education. They learn to ask questions like, "Where is God in all of this?"

"How might I have contributed to the dynamic I'm experiencing?" and "What might this mean about my calling?" In other words, a negative experience in field education can still provide great learning, painful as the year might be for all parties involved.

Some seminary courses are content-oriented, where the purpose of the course is to transmit to the student a body of knowledge she or he will need in ministry. Other courses are process-oriented, where the goal of the experience has more to do with internal growth and professional maturation than information sharing. This internal growth favors intentionality in goal setting, self-assessment, solicitation of feedback, and accountability. Through practicing these important leadership development functions in field education, students not only grow as ministry professionals but also develop habits for a lifetime. The assessment process that accompanies and deepens learning in field education can provide a first foray into a whole new way of thinking about a life in ministry.

For Supervisor- Mentors and Field Educators

Imagine that a supervisor-mentor or lay leader in a congregation charged with supporting a field education student has helped a student to develop a goal and related objectives and is supporting the student as he or she implements the learning plan. The supervisor-mentor soon must turn toward considering formal evaluation processes. The more involved the supervisor-mentor was in the early and intermediate steps in the process, the more ready she or he will be for this phase. Yet so often supervisor-mentors are misinformed or misled to believe that their assessment role begins, rather than culminates, in formal evaluation processes. From where does this misinformation come? How can we in partnership create a learning environment that helps assessment to be not only a growth experience but also an integrated and logical step in the wider arc of theological field education?

Those who support students in field education find themselves caught between two attitudes about assessment. On one end of the spectrum, supervisor-mentors in particular feel pressure to cheerlead and comfort, believing that anything they say to their student that does not affirm will cause conflict not worth their time and energy. On the other end, supervisor-mentors feel pressure to weed out students who are not emotionally or intellectually capable of ministry. I constantly say to the supervisors with whom I work, "You are there to support students' learning, and therefore you should measure every comment you make and every conclusion you draw against the question, Will this action further the students' learning?" Even with an emphasis on student learning, however, controversy surrounds student learning assessment for a variety of reasons. In her book on evaluating ministry programs, pastoral theologian Kathleen Cahalan lists "some common attitudes about evaluation: it consists of immediate feedback after the event; it is extra work added on to an already full agenda; it requires experts; and it's challenging and possibly dangerous."[1] If misunderstanding the nature of evaluation and assessment were not enough, professional educators tend to resist standardizing learning assessment for both pedagogical and political reasons. In an article "A Pedagogical Straitjacket" in the respected weekly paper *The Chronicle of Higher Education*, higher education observer Laurie Fendrich calls student learning assessment "grotesque, unintentional parodies of both social science and 'accountability.'"[2] Fendrich writes of faculty members she knows who consider the movement in education toward outcomes-based student learning assessment, where change in the student is given more attention in evaluation than the practices of the teacher, to be "downright scary."[3] In such an atmosphere of suspicion and anxiety about evaluation, assessment is not commonly understood as an accountability process intended to foster student learning.

Therefore, supervisor-mentors must intentionally create an atmosphere where partners in student learning have a healthy attitude toward assessment. Organizations that are, attitudinally and theologically, best able to treat assessment for what it is, a crucial and integral infrastructure for supporting student learning in ministry, can be identified by four markers.

MARKER 1

Feedback is a teaching tool built into the interactions supervisor-mentors and congregational leaders have with students and is offered regularly. The goal of feedback is learning, not judgment or the joy of being right.

As in most of life, bringing up concerns as they arise rather than allowing them to fester is a good practice for sustaining healthy relationships. Unfortunately for student learning, supervisor-mentors and congregational leaders sometimes "pull their punches," hesitating to share feedback with students about how they are coming across and how they are performing in their ministry tasks. They wait until formal evaluations come along, and then they overload students with more feedback than students can process, and learning gets drowned out by defensiveness and anxiety.

The best way to create a feedback-friendly environment is to set up the expectation from the beginning that feedback will be part of the regularly scheduled interactions of all field education relationships. By bringing this up before a concern has arisen, the student comes to expect both positive affirmation and corrective coaching and is prepared for that form of communication. In setting that expectation, it is useful to ask the students questions like, "What kind of feedback would be most helpful for you?" "In the past, what style of delivering feedback has been most helpful, and most harmful, to your learning?" "What have been your past experiences with feedback in school and in work?" Giving the student an opportunity to help set the tone around feedback sharing, before an issue comes up rather than during a crisis, helps the medicine of hard conversations to go down easier later.

Supervisor-mentors can sometimes be critical of students for not taking feedback better, but it is important for them to remember that internalizing feedback takes time. Sometimes, the supervisor-mentor shares a concern with a student that she or he has been thinking about for weeks or months, but then is surprised when the student, with no prior thought about the matter, does not immediately grasp or own the problem. In a feedback-friendly environment, students are given time to digest information about how they are performing or coming across. Written reports include information about feedback that the supervisor-mentor has shared with the student, and also information about how the supervisor-mentor and student have together discussed and processed that feedback. Written reports are not used to offer critique for the first time but rather as a means of chronicling concerns and how the student has received those concerns.

MARKER 2

Conversation is theologically grounded; all partners in learning believe that actions have deeper meanings worthy of exploration.

The tasks that students perform in field education are inductive, meaning that they "move from the particular or the specific to the general or theoretical."[4] In theological field education, the specifics are ministry events, and the theoretical grounding for meaning making is "theo-logy," God-knowing. As students implement their plans for learning, they discover gaps between what they know and what they do, what they believe and how they behave. In her article "Attending to the Gaps between Beliefs and Practices," doctrinal theologian Amy Plantinga Pauw writes that these gaps are where real theology takes place.[5] I argue that in this gap the supervisor-mentor sits with the student in theological reflection sessions, making sense of what must change: their beliefs or their way of life and ministry? By searching for theological meaning when events deal the student surprises or setbacks, students not only become more grounded in their beliefs but from each ministry task they perform they also harvest meaning for future use.

MARKER 3

No one in the setting behaves as though she or he is beyond learning or is "fully evolved." Adults in the setting embrace a positive attitude toward lifelong learning.

My observation is that supervisor-mentors who work well with students seem to appreciate lifelong learning. They view learning for ministry as a journey, not a destination, and they often comment on how much they learn themselves by working with a student minister. Besides showing up for continuing education when it is available, how does a supervisor-mentor with a positive attitude toward learning demonstrate that passion? What are the habits of those who see themselves as both learners and teachers in their work as supervisor-mentors?

First, such supervisor-mentors tend to have a self-effacing sense of humor. They might use their own foibles as examples to soften the blow when the student has learned something the hard way. In a healthy rather than a needy way, they give their students a peek into their own insecurities in order to model to the student that all ministerial leaders are works in progress, constantly growing and improving.

Second, supervisor-mentors with a positive attitude toward learning do not show surprise or frustration when their student does not already know something. Comments such as, "They didn't teach you that in class?" or "Seriously? You've never been in a pulpit?" make students anxious and betray a misunderstanding of the role of field education in the life of the minister in formation: Of course there are things the student has never done. They are, after all, students! Demonstrating excitement at having the opportunity to witness the student doing something new, rather than astonishment or even disgust, marks a positive attitude about learning.

Third, the supervisor with a healthy attitude toward learning does not vent anger toward the student. Many supervisor-mentors take a risk when they work with a student. If the supervisor-mentor is a pastor, she or he must give up some control and power when giving over ministry tasks to the student. Sometimes, the supervisor-mentor fears that a congregant will be alienated by a choice the student makes or visitors will not pursue membership if they happen to come when a nervous, quavering, well-intentioned novice is in a primary public role. This anxiety can sometimes lead the supervisor-mentor to feel angry, protective of the congregation, and concerned about his or her own position and its security. At times like this, learning-oriented supervisor-mentors seek out supervision themselves in order to work out their feelings, and they focus their work with their students on his or her learning, not venting their own frustrations.

When supervisor-mentors model to students humility about their own learning gaps and point out the ways in which even the institutions where the students are learning are still living into their callings, supervisor-mentors create an atmosphere where students do not feel singled out as the only ones engaged in assessment. This creates an atmosphere in which formal evaluation goes down easier than in a setting where the student is expected to grow while all other parties perceive themselves to be perfectly fully evolved.

MARKER 4

Expectations of one another are transparent, negotiated, and shared. When an expectation is violated, people show generosity toward one another, first assuming that an expectation must be visited or revisited before laying blame.

In Jill Hudson's book *When Better Isn't Enough: Evaluation Tools for the 21st-Century Church,* Hudson presents twelve standards for pastors in light of which their performance should be evaluated.[6] She takes the time to do so because, as she lays out throughout the book, we live in a complex and quickly changing time where standards of effectiveness are not agreed upon mutually without effort. Irony abounds: without standards, evaluation is not possible, but there is no standardized list for standards!

In congregations, many mental models coexist regarding expectations of the pastor. Each member, each leader, and the pastor him- or herself has ideas about what defines effectiveness, which come only in part from formal descriptions of roles. The rest of the expectations come from experiences in other settings, such as other churches, our families of origin, and our current families. Congregants gather input from culture and other sources, and from all of these different sources they form personal impressions of what they expect from their ministers. Therefore, without intentional discussion about expectations for a student minister in particular, disappointment is inevitable, on all sides; for everyone involved in the ministry setting has a different set of impressions—tacit or spoken—about what ministers are supposed to be and do.

At the same time, anticipating every potential situation is not possible. Therefore, beyond transparency about expectations, partners in student learning must practice forgiveness and grace. When the student fails to meet an expectation or intentionally operates outside agreed-upon duties, supervisor-mentors must address the situation. Entering conversations like these with an assumption that the student meant no harm, a predisposition toward believing that expectations played at least a partial role in the issue at hand, and a willingness to revisit expectations as part of addressing the situation creates an atmosphere where learning—rather than simply hard feelings—follows mistakes.

That said, students often have difficulty owning their actions when their intentions were good; they sometimes respond to their supervisor-mentor's concern with the attitude that their intentions and not their actions are their only responsibility. The supervisor-mentor must, in such cases, help students to understand that in the congregation, their intentions are actually less important than their actions. This is one key way in which experiential education is different from classroom learning: It affects other people. Affirming intentions is one way to soften the blow when addressing unmet expectations, or wrongly met expectations, but that affirmation cannot be the end of the conversation if our hope is that students learn.

THE MARKERS IN PRACTICE

These four customs of an assessment-friendly learning environment might seem easy to live out, but when applied to a real ministry situation, we can see that they at times run counter to the initially obvious course of action. Imagine this scenario: You are a supervisor-mentor in a nursing home chaplaincy program, and the student with whom you are working loves to joke around. He calls every resident he meets "buddy" if a man, "sweetheart" if a woman, but with the staff he uses their given names. Residents notice this and comment upon it, some positively, some negatively: "No one has called me 'sweetheart' since my husband died"; "He and I just met—he's no 'buddy' of mine." How might a learning environment that encompasses all four of the named markers help the supervisor-mentor address such an issue so that it becomes a learning experience for the student?

Marker 1: *Sharing feedback is built in.* If feedback sharing is the custom of the setting, the way the student is addressing residents would come up right away, in the first supervision session after you heard about his use of nicknames. You would have to protect the privacy of those who brought the issue to you, but you would not wait to talk about it until a crisis arose. In the interest of focusing on learning rather than simply performing a single task, you would think in advance about how you might frame issues in such a way that the student would learn something from the encounter.

Marker 2: *Theological grounding and meaning making.* You would talk with the student about the meaning of names in the Bible, in our baptisms, in the life of the faithful person. You would ask the student what names mean to him and how affectionate names had been part of his life before coming to this setting.

Marker 3: *We are all learning.* You would contextualize your critique of the student's practice by talking about what you have learned, sometimes the hard way and sometimes the easy way, from working in a nursing home setting. You would help the student to think in different ways about nicknames; might the student come on his own to the conclusion that the nicknames he has chosen could be interpreted as patronizing, or sexualized? If he does not come to this realization on his own, you might point out the flaws in the nicknames he has been using, tempering this critique with thoughtful consideration of what it is like for a person with no prior experience with a population to work with them.

Marker 4: *Expectations are transparent, and when violated, we are generous.* You would reset the expectations with the student about what he ought to call residents, certainly. But you would do so while fully owning that this was an unanticipated issue, that you believe he meant no harm, and that therefore he is not in trouble. In the future, were such issues to reemerge, the conversation might take on a different tone, but in these first conversations, one must assume the student did not know what he did not know.

Forming Habits of Reflective Practice

In his book *Educating the Reflective Practitioner*, education for the professions scholar Donald Schön writes about three ways in which a person learns a profession: developing skills, learning to *think like* a professional in the field, and forming habits of reflective practice.[7] He argues that all three are important, but the last—reflective practice—is most needed today. The world is changing so quickly that it is impossible to anticipate the challenges those being formed for ministry today will face tomorrow. Therefore, developing the ability to learn from experience over the course of a lifetime is perhaps the loftiest goal of assessment practices in field education.

As students in collaboration with their partners set goals, craft plans, implement those plans, and reflect on their accomplishments, they set a lifelong pattern for learning. The pattern not only helps them to grow continually in their ministries but it also helps them to lead institutions. For churches, schools, and agencies also must set goals, live into them, and take time to assess whether they are hitting the mark. Outcomes-based assessment is a hot topic in education and religious organizations today, but the sad truth is that few leaders have conducted an assessment process in their own lives; how are they then to help the organization they lead to do so? The hope is that your experience—whether you are a student, congregational leader, or supervisor-mentor—will equip you to think in a new way about the work you do.

This chapter has offered a set of planning and evaluation practices for theological field education. The practices come together in the form of intentional-field-education student-learning assessment, the infrastructure that undergirds a student's growth and formation through theological field education. When sequenced and pursued with intentionality, these practices account for the difference between what was once called *field work*, or task-oriented ministry apprenticeships, and *field education*, where students not only learn how to perform tasks but also grow as people and professionals.

Notes

CHAPTER 1: WHAT IS THEOLOGICAL FIELD EDUCATION?

1. Rev. John Smith served as a Reformed Church in America minister of Word and Sacrament in rural congregations in Illinois and Iowa during his long career. He died during the writing of this book. Other names have been changed to preserve confidentiality.
2. Charles Feilding, *Theological Education* 3, no. 1 (Autumn 1966).
3. Ibid., 13.
4. Ibid., 233.
5. Erik H. Erikson, *Identity and the Life Cycle* (New York: Norton, 1980). See chart on p. 129.
6. Parker Palmer, *Let Your Life Speak: Listening for the Voice of Vocation* (San Francisco: Jossey-Bass, 2000), 11.
7. Edward Cell, "Mapping Experiences," in *Learning to Learn from Experience* (Albany: State University of New York Press, 1984), chap. 3. Cell also explores resistance to learning.
8. "Pastoral and Ecclesial Imagination," in *For Life Abundant: Practical Theology, Theological Education, and Christian Ministry*, ed. Dorothy C. Bass and Craig Dykstra (Grand Rapids: Eerdmans, 2008), 51. Craig Dykstra's chapter is the fruit of sustained thinking about ministerial formation, thriving communities of faith, and theological education.
9. Eduard C. Lindeman, *The Meaning of Adult Education* (Montreal: Harvest House, 1961), 6.
10. S. Joseph Levine, *Getting to the Core: Reflections on Teaching and Learning* (Okemos, MI: LearnerAssociates.net, 2005), 101–2.
11. Donald A. Schön, *Educating the Reflective Practitioner* (San Francisco: Jossey-Bass, 1987), 22–40.
12. Ibid., 103.

13. Laurent A. Parks Daloz, et al., *Common Fire: Leading Lives of Commitment in a Complex World* (Boston: Beacon Press, 1996), 44–46. Parks Daloz and the other authors engage important questions about formation for young adults who will be capable of making meaning and keeping significant commitments.

14. A portion of the congregational prayer offered by intern Andrew Mead at Third Reformed Church, Holland, Michigan, in worship on Sunday, February 28, 2010.

15. George Hunter, *Theological Field Education* (Newton Centre, MA: The Boston Theological Institute, 1977), 1.

16. In-service training conducted at Western Theological Seminary on February 2, 2010, by Charlene Jin Lee.

17. Amy Gostkowski, "What Makes a Great Coach?" *USA Hockey*, October 2009, 36.

18. Max De Pree, *Leadership Jazz* (New York: Doubleday, 1992), 102–3.

19. Surveys conducted among field education participants 2005–2008 at Western Theological Seminary, Holland, Michigan.

20. Lee Knefelkamp, Carole Widick, Clyde A. Parker, "Erik Erikson and Psychosocial Development," in *New Directions for Student Services: Applying New Developmental Findings* (San Francisco: Jossey-Bass, 1978), 6–7.

21. Schön, *Reflective Practitioner*, 163.

22. *Becoming a Pastor: Reflections on the Transition into Ministry* (Herndon, VA: Alban Institute, 2008), 13.

23. Ibid., 14.

24. Ibid., 30.

25. Ibid., 39.

26. John E. Paver, *Theological Reflection and Education for Ministry: The Search for Integration in Theology*, Explorations in Practical, Pastoral, and Empirical Theology (Burlington, VT: Ashgate Publishing, 2006), 3.

27. Michael Pollan, *The Botany of Desire* (New York: Random House, Inc., 2001), 10.

CHAPTER 2: THE ART OF SUPERVISION AND FORMATION

1. Haiku composed by Bill Maroon, published in *Teaching and Religious Imagination,* Maria Harris (San Fransisco: Harper & Row, 1991), 23.

2. Janet L. Miller names the unexpected—often received as troubling—interjection of the private self in public, *scholarly discourse.* In *Sounds of Silence Breaking: Women, Autobiography, Curriculum* (New York: Peter Lang, 2005), 87–105, Miller speaks to this "surprise" of the self in academia as

a welcoming and necessary presence: it is a tool for humanizing a game in "colorless abstractions and obfuscating jargon." Here, I contextualize Miller's terminology to describe how one might re-see otherness when one is able to recognize the familiar human brokenness beneath superficial interactions.

3. Ibid., 25.

4. Lao Tzu, *The Tao Te Ching of Lao Tzu*, trans. Brian Browne Walker (New York: St. Martin's Griffin, 1996), 14.

5. Madeline Grumet, "Existential and Phenomenological Foundations of Autobiographical Methods," in *Understanding Curriculum as Phenomenological and Deconstructed Text*, ed. William Pinar and William Reynolds (New York: Teachers College Press, 1992), 29.

6. I borrow this word and its represented concept from Paulo Freire. Freire describes the ongoing formation of the contextual self as awareness of our unfinishedness in his book *Pedagogy of Freedom* (Lanham, MD: Rowman & Littlefield, 1998), 51. He writes, "I hold that my own unity and identity, in regard to others and to the world, constitutes my essential and irrepeatable way of experiencing myself as a cultural, historical, and unfinished being in the world, simultaneously conscious of my unfinishedness."

7. Society of the Promotion of Buddhism, *The Teaching of Buddha* (Tokyo: Kosaido Printing, 1998).

8. See Mary Aswell Doll, *Like Letters in Running Water: A Mythopoetics of Curriculum* (New York: Routledge, 2001).

CHAPTER 3: MINISTERIAL REFLECTION

1. These are *Educating the Reflective Practitioner* and *The Reflective Practitioner*. Schön also coauthored works with Chris Argyris, including *Theory in Practice*. Schön studied how professionals in many fields learn to act in the midst of complicated situations, informed by theory but also practicing the artistry of design in relation to specific situations.

CHAPTER 4: THE USE OF CASE STUDIES IN FIELD EDUCATION

1. Throughout this chapter, the sections about analyzing, writing, and presenting a case have been adapted from Jeanene Reese, ed., *A Case Method Approach to Teaching and Learning: Exploring Applications for Teaching in*

Academic and Community Contexts (Abilene, TX: Association for Case Teaching, 2006).

2. William H. Willimon, ed., *The Sunday After Tuesday: College Pulpits Respond to 9/11* (Nashville: Abingdon Press, 2002).

3. Kenneth Burke, *A Grammar of Motives* (New York: Prentice-Hall, 1945). See also Burke's *A Rhetoric of Motives* (New York: Prentice-Hall, 1950).

CHAPTER 5: THE POWER OF REFLECTING WITH PEERS

1. Sample peer-group covenant from Western Theological Seminary, Holland, Michigan.

2. Susan Scott, *Fierce Conversations: Achieving Success at Work and in Life, One Conversation at a Time* (New York: Viking Penguin, 2002). Reprinted with permission.

CHAPTER 6: THE FORMING WORK OF CONGREGATIONS

1. Robert J. Schreiter, "Theology in the Congregation," in *Studying Congregations: A New Handbook*, ed. Nancy T. Ammerman et al. (Nashville: Abingdon Press, 1998), 23.

2. Ibid., 31.

3. Thomas H. Groome, "Theology on Our Feet: A Revisionist Pedagogy for Healing the Gap between Academia and Ecclesia," in *Formation and Reflection: The Promise of Practical Theology*, ed. Lewis S. Mudge and James N. Poling (Philadelphia: Fortress Press, 1987), 57. Italics added for emphasis.

4. See Ammerman et al., eds., *Studying Congregations*. An earlier edition used four slightly different "frames "or categories for congregational study: identity, programs, processes, and social contexts. See Jackson Carroll et al., eds., *Handbook for Congregational Studies* (Nashville: Abingdon, 1986).

5. H. Richard Niebuhr, *Christ and Culture* (New York: Harper & Row, 1951).

6. David A. Roozen, William McKinney, and Jackson W. Carroll, *Varieties of Religious Presence: Mission in Public Life* (New York: Pilgrim Press, 1984).

7. John P. Kretzmann and John McKnight, *Building Communities from the Inside Out: A Path toward Finding and Mobilizing a Community's As-*

sets (Evanston, IL: Asset-Based Community Development Institute, 1993). See also Luther Snow, *The Power of Asset Mapping: How Your Congregation Can Act on Its Gifts* (Herndon, VA: Alban Institute, 2004).

8. Percept website, www.perceptgroup.com.

9. Visions-Decisions website, www.visions-decisions.com.

10. U.S. Census Bureau website, www.census.gov.

11. Jackson W. Carroll, Carl S. Dudley, and William McKinney, eds., *Handbook for Congregational Studies* (Nashville: Abingdon Press, 1986), 81.

12. Ammerman et al., *Studying Congregations*, 107ff.

13. Kenneth Thomas, *Handbook of Industrial and Organizational Psychology* (Chicago: Rand McNally, 1976).

14. For additional resources in understanding congregational conflict, see Speed B. Leas, *Discover Your Conflict Management Style* (Herndon, VA: Alban Institute, 1997); and Peter L. Steinke, *How Your Church Family Works: Understanding Congregations as Emotional Systems* (Herndon, VA: Alban Institute, 1993).

15. Daniel Goleman, Richard Boyatzis, and Annie McKee, *Primal Leadership: Realizing the Power of Emotional Intelligence* (Boston: Harvard Business School Press, 2002), 51–69.

16. Process adapted from William T. Pyle and Mary Alice Seals, eds., *Experiencing Ministry Supervision: A Field-Based Approach* (Nashville: Broadman & Holman, 1995), 77.

17. See R. Leon Carroll Jr., "Generative Teaching Congregations: Colleagues in Theological Field Education" (unpublished paper, 2004).

CHAPTER 7: SELF-CARE AND COMMUNITY

1. G. Lloyd Rediger, *Fit to Be a Pastor: A Call to Physical, Mental, and Spiritual Fitness* (Louisville, KY: Westminster John Knox Press, 2000), xi.

2. Roy M. Oswald, *Clergy Self-Care: Finding a Balance for Effective Ministry* (Herndon, VA: Alban Institute, 1991), 3.

3. Jaco J. Hamman, *Becoming a Pastor: Forming Self and Soul for Ministry* (Cleveland: Pilgrim Press, 2007), 179.

4. Oswald, 143.

5. Find the research here: Richard J. Krejcir, "Statistics on Pastors," ChurchLeadership.org, The Francis A. Schaeffer Institute of Church Leadership Development, http://www.churchleadership.org/apps/articles/default.asp?articleid=42347&columnid=4545.

6. Norman Wirzba, *Living the Sabbath: Discovering the Rhythms of Rest and Delight*, The Christian Practice of Everyday Life (Grand Rapids: Brazos Press, 2006), 20.

7. Allison M. Moore, *Clergy Moms: A Survival Guide to Balancing Family and Congregation* (New York: Seabury Books, 2008), 36–37.

8. Donald R. Hands and Wayne L. Fehr, *Spiritual Wholeness for Clergy: A New Psychology of Intimacy with God, Self, and Others* (Herndon, VA: Alban Institute, 1993), 68.

9. Ibid., 45.

10. For more on psychological defense mechanisms, see George E. Vaillant, *The Wisdom of the Ego* (Cambridge, MA: Harvard University Press, 1993).

11. See Rochelle Melander and Harold Eppley, *The Spiritual Leader's Guide to Self-Care* (Herndon, VA: Alban Institute, 2002).

CHAPTER 8: MINISTERIAL ETHICS

1. Richard M. Gula, *Ethics in Pastoral Ministry* (New York: Paulist Press, 1996), 1–3.

2. Ibid., 16.

3. Joseph L. Allen, *Love and Conflict: A Covenantal Model of Christian Ethics* (Lanham, MD: University Press of America, 1995), 20.

4. Barbara J. Blodgett, *Lives Entrusted: An Ethic of Trust for Ministry* (Minneapolis: Fortress Press, 2008), 50.

5. Joseph E. Bush Jr., *Gentle Shepherding: Pastoral Ethics and Leadership* (St. Louis: Chalice Press, 2006), 110.

6. Gaylord Noyce, *Pastoral Ethics: Professional Responsibilities of the Clergy* (Nashville: Abingdon Press, 1988), 91.

7. Karen Lebacqz, *Professional Ethics: Power and Paradox* (Nashville: Abingdon Press, 1985), 82.

8. See Blodgett, *Lives Entrusted*, chapter 2, "Confidentiality."

9. A note to supervisor-mentors: Your two covenantal relationships are to your intern and the theological field educator, and you will want to keep open lines of communication with each. If you receive information about your intern that you think is relevant for the field educator to know in his or her position as someone responsible for the student's welfare, you should share it. The information might affect their life as a student at the school and as a person preparing for ministry. Likewise, the field educator should share with you any information you deserve to know. However,

the field educator may be constrained by privacy laws in sharing certain confidential information with you. The program should have clear policies about information sharing and access. These might vary by school and by denomination (if relevant). All policies should be shared with you in the program's written materials and during the training you participate in to become a supervisor-mentor in the program.

CHAPTER 9 : LANGUAGE AND LEADERSHIP

1. Robert Kegan and Lisa Laskow Lahey, *How the Way We Talk Can Change the Way We Work: Seven Languages of Transformation* (San Francisco: Jossey-Bass, 2001), 8.
2. This saying can be found at White Bison Center for the Wellbriety Movement website, http://www.whitebison.org/meditation/data/1212.med.
3. David D. Day, Michelle M. Harrison, and Stanley M. Halpin, *An Integrative Approach to Leader Development: Connecting Adult Development, Identity, and Expertise* (New York: Psychology Press Taylor & Francis Group, 2009), xii.
4. Ronald A. Heifetz, *Leadership without Easy Answers* (Cambridge: Bellknap Press, 2001).
5. Robert Kegan and Lisa Laskow Lahey, *Immunity to Change: How to Overcome It and Unlock the Potential in Yourself and Your Organization* (Boston: Harvard Business Press, 2009), 29.
6. Ibid., x.
7. Permission granted to use four column exercise through Lisa Lahey, copyright Minds at Work.
8. For other examples of how this four column exercise can be used in a pastoral setting, see Lorraine Ste-Marie, *Beyond Words: A New Language for a Changing Church* (Ottawa, ON: Novalis, 2008).
9. Kegan and Lahey, *How the Way We Talk*, 13.
10. Kegan and Lahey, *Immunity to Change*, 231–33.
11. Kegan and Lahey, *How the Way We Talk*, 33–46.
12. Kegan and Lahey, *Immunity to Change*, 233–35.
13. Kegan and Lahey, *How the Way We Talk*, 47.
14. Ibid.
15. Charlene P. E. Burns, "Cognitive Dissonance Theory and the Induced-Compliance Paradigm: Concerns for Teaching Religious Studies," *Teaching Theology and Religion* 9, no. 1 (January 2006): 3–8.

16. Kegan and Lahey, *How the Way We Talk*, 58.
17. Kegan and Lahey, *Immunity to Change*, 236–46.
18. Kegan and Lahey, *How the Way We Talk*, 67.
19. Ibid., 74.
20. Ibid., 91.
21. Ibid., 121.
22. Ibid., 134.
23. Ibid., 141.
24. David D. Day et al., *An Integrative Approach to Leader Development*, xii.

CHAPTER 10: CONSIDERATIONS FOR CROSS-CULTURAL PLACEMENT

1. Brian K. Blount, gen. ed., *True to Our Native Land: An African American New Testament Commentary* (Minneapolis: Fortress Press, 2007), 268.
2. Pema Chodron, *What Happens When Things Fall Apart: Heart Advice for Difficult Times* (Boston: Shambhala Publications, 1997), 18.
3. Eric Law, Training Module 1 and Training Module 2, Kaleidoscope Institute, Los Angeles, November 4–9, 2007.
4. Eric Law, "What Is Competent Leadership in a Diverse, Changing World?"; Kaleidoscope Institute website, http://216.104.171.229/ki/.
5. Blount, *True to Our Native Land*, 268.
6. Carl G. Jung, *The Practice of Psychotherapy* (London: Routledge & Kegan Paul, 1954), 68.
7. Jaco Hamman, *Becoming a Pastor: Forming Self and Soul for Ministry* (Cleveland: Pilgrim Press, 2007).

CHAPTER 11: ASSESSMENT AND THEOLOGICAL FIELD EDUCATION

1. Kathleen A. Cahalan, *Projects That Matter: Successful Planning and Evaluation for Religious Organizations* (Herndon, VA: Alban Institute, 2003), 31.
2. Laurie Fendrich, "A Pedagogical Straitjacket," *The Chronicle of Higher Education*, June 8, 2007, B6.
3. Ibid.

4. Jane Vella, Paula Berardinelli, and Jim Burrow, *How Do They Know They Know? Evaluating Adult Learning* (San Francisco: Jossey-Bass, 1998), 106.

5. Amy Plantinga Pauw, "Attending to the Gaps between Beliefs and Practices," in *Practicing Theology: Beliefs and Practices in Christian Life*, ed. Miroslav Volf and Dorothy C. Bass (Grand Rapids: Wm. B. Eerdmans, 2002), 33–48. Note: This line of argument about professional learning attending to the gaps between espoused beliefs and lived practices can also be found in Chris Argyris and Donald A. Schön, *Theory in Practice: Increasing Professional Effectiveness* (San Francisco: Jossey-Bass, 1974), 6–7.

6. Jill M. Hudson, *When Better Isn't Enough: Evaluation Tools for the 21st-Century Church* (Herndon, VA: Alban Institute, 2004).

7. Donald A. Schön, *Educating the Reflective Practitioner* (San Francisco: Jossey-Bass, 1987), 39–40.

Bibliography

Ammerman, Nancy T., Jackson W. Carroll, Carl S. Dudley, and William McKinney, eds. *Studying Congregations: A New Handbook.* Nashville: Abingdon Press, 1998.

Anderson, Ray Sherman. *Self-Care: A Theology of Personal Empowerment and Spiritual Healing.* Wheaton, IL: Victor Books, 1995.

Argyris, Chris, and Donald Schön. *Theory in Practice: Increasing Professional Effectiveness.* San Francisco: Jossey-Bass, 1974.

Bass, Dorothy, and Craig Dykstra, eds. *For Life Abundant: Practical Theology, Theological Education, and Christian Ministry.* Grand Rapids: Eerdmans, 2008.

Blodgett, Barbara J. *Lives Entrusted: An Ethic of Trust for Ministry.* Minneapolis: Fortress Press, 2008.

Bush, Jr., Joseph E. *Gentle Shepherding: Pastoral Ethics and Leadership.* St. Louis: Chalice Press, 2006.

Conde-Frazier, Elizabeth, S. Steve Kang, and Gary A. Parrett. *A Many Colored Kingdom: Multicultural Dynamics for Spiritual Formation.* Grand Rapids: Baker, 2004.

Emerson, Michael O., and Christian Smith. *Divided by Faith: Evangelical Religion and the Problem of Race in America.* New York: Oxford University Press, 2000.

Esterline, David V., and Ogbu U. Kalu, eds. *Shaping Beloved Community: Multicultural Theological Education.* Louisville: Westminster John Knox Press, 2006.

Foster, Charles R., Lisa E. Dahill, Lawrence A. Goleman, and Barbara Wang Tolentino. *Educating Clergy: Teaching Practices and Pastoral Imagination.* San Francisco: Jossey-Bass, 2006.

Freire, Paulo. *Pedagogy of Freedom.* Lanham, MD: Rowman & Littlefield, 2001.

Garrido, Ann. *A Concise Guide to Supervising a Ministry Student.* Notre Dame, IN: Ave Maria Press, 2008.

Garvin, David A. "Making the Case: Professional Education for the World of Practice," in *Harvard Magazine* 106, no. 1 (Sept–Oct 2003): 56–65, 107. Available from Harvard Magazine, http://www.harvardmagazine.com/on-line/090322.html.

Groome, Thomas H. *Christian Religious Education: Sharing Our Story and Vision.* San Francisco: Harper & Row, 1980.

Gula, Richard M. *Ethics in Pastoral Ministry* (New York: Paulist Press, 1996).

Heifetz, Ronald A. *Leadership without Easy Answers.* Cambridge: Bellknap Press, 2001.

Hooks, Bell. *Teaching to Transgress.* New York: Routledge, 1994.

Kegan, Robert, and Lisa Laskow Lahey. *How the Way We Talk Can Change the Way We Work: Seven Languages of Transformation.* San Francisco: Jossey-Bass, 2001.

———. *Immunity to Change: How to Overcome It and Unlock the Potential in Yourself and Your Organization.* Boston: Harvard Business Press, 2009.

Kretzmann, John P., and John McKnight. *Building Communities from the Inside Out: A Path toward Finding and Mobilizing a Community's Assets.* Evanston, IL: Asset-Based Community Development Institute, 1993.

Lave, Jean, and Etienne Wenger. *Situated Learning.* New York: Cambridge University Press, 2009.

Law, Eric H. F. *The Bush Was Blazing but Not Consumed: Developing a Multicultural Community through Dialogue and Liturgy.* St. Louis: Chalice Press, 1996.

Lehr, J. Fred. *Clergy Burnout: Recovering from the 70-Hour Week . . . and Other Self-Defeating Practices*, Prisms. Minneapolis: Fortress Press, 2006.

Lewis, G. Douglass. *Resolving Church Conflicts: A Case Study Approach for Local Congregations.* San Francisco: Harper & Row, 1981.

Mahan, Jeffrey, Barbara Troxell, and Carol Allen. *Shared Wisdom: A Guide to Case Study Reflection in Ministry.* Nashville: Abingdon Press, 1993.

Palmer, Parker. *To Know as We Are Known.* New York: HarperOne, 1993.

Rediger, G. Lloyd. *Beyond the Scandals: A Guide to Healthy Sexuality for Clergy*, Prisms. Minneapolis: Fortress Press, 2003.

Richardson, Ronald W. *Becoming a Healthier Pastor: Family Systems Theory and the Pastor's Own Family*, Creative Pastoral Care and Counseling Series. Minneapolis: Fortress Press, 2005.

Schön, Donald A. *Educating the Reflective Practitioner: Toward a New Design for Teaching and Learning in the Professions.* San Francisco: Jossey-Bass, 1987.

———. *The Reflective Practitioner: How Professionals Think in Action.* New York: Basic Books, 1983.

Ste-Marie, Lorraine. *Beyond Words: A New Language for a Changing Church.* Ottawa, ON: Novalis, 2008.

Swetland, Kenneth L. *The Hidden World of the Pastor: Case Studies on Personal Issues of Real Pastors.* Grand Rapids: Baker Books, 1995; and *Facing Messy Stuff in the Church: Case Studies for Pastors and Congregations.* Grand Rapids: Kregel, 2005.

Vella, Jane, Paula Berardinelli, and Jim Burrow. *How Do They Know They Know? Evaluating Adult Learning.* San Francisco: Jossey-Bass, 1998.

Williams, Brian A. *The Potter's Rib: Mentoring for Pastoral Formation.* Vancouver, BC: Regent College Publishing, 2005.

Contributors

Barbara Blodgett is currently minister for vocation and formation for the United Church of Christ. She previously served for ten years as Director of Supervised Ministries at Yale Divinity School. Her research interests include ministry ethics, pedagogy, and practices for ministerial formation.

Lee Carroll is associate professor emeritus of supervised ministry at Columbia Theological Seminary, Decatur, Georgia, having retired in 2009. He served as a field educator for twenty-six years. He is an ordained minister of Word and Sacrament of the Presbyterian Church (USA) and previously served as a minister with three congregations. He is married to Betty Wilby Carroll and has two grown children and three grandchildren.

Emily Click is assistant dean for ministry studies and director of field education at Harvard Divinity School. She writes and teaches on theological field education in relationship to major education theories. Other interests include mentoring, leadership, and practical theology.

Sarah B. Drummond is the associate dean of the faculty and assistant professor of ministerial leadership at Andover Newton Theological School. She directs Andover Newton's historic Field Education Program and the seminary's Master of Divinity program. She is an ordained minister in the United Church of Christ.

Donna Duensing has served as a theological field educator for twenty years. She is currently serving as deployed associate for contextual education at Pacific Lutheran Theological Seminary, Berkeley, California.

Matthew Floding is director of formation for ministry and associate professor of Christian ministry at Western Theological Seminary in Holland, Michigan. His field education interests focus on the intersection of pastoral theology, experiential education, and leadership theory in support of ministerial formation. He is an ordained minister of Word and Sacrament in the Reformed Church in America.

Jaco Hamman is professor of pastoral care and counseling at Western Theological Seminary, Holland, Michigan. He completed his theological education at the Universities of Port Elizabeth and Stellenbosch, both in South Africa, and at Princeton Theological Seminary. An ordained Reformed Church in America minister, Hamman completed clinical training in pastoral psychotherapy, marriage and family therapy, and group therapy at The Blanton-Peale Graduate Institute, New York.

Charlene Jin Lee is assistant professor of Christian education and director of student formation at San Francisco Theological Seminary, where she teaches practical theology. Interested in examining the sociopolitical dimensions of being church in the world, Lee focuses her research on contextual theologies, narrative theory, and identity formation.

Joanne Lindstrom is the Jean and Frank Mohr Director of Field Studies and Experiential Education, assistant professor of ministry at McCormick Theological Seminary in Chicago. She teaches the required concurrent course, "Reflection on the Practice of Ministry" and elective courses in spirituality. Reverend Lindstrom is an ordained minister of American Baptist Churches USA and has served as associate minister of the First Baptist Church, Chicago, for fifteen years.

Lorraine Ste-Marie is assistant professor in practical theology at St. Paul University in Ottawa, Ontario. She teaches in the Master of Pastoral Theology, Master of Arts in Counseling and Spirituality, and the Doctor of Ministry programs. Her areas of research and writing focus on developmental learning in pastoral leadership education.

Tim Sensing is the director of academic services and associate professor of ministry and homiletics for the Graduate School of Theology at Abilene Christian University. While Tim's primary research interests pertain to homiletics, his secondary areas of interest are research methodologies and pedagogy. In the area of pedagogy, he concentrates on contextual education, distance education, and case teaching.